THE POWER OF
Movement

How to Avoid Stagnation and Achieve Your Dreams

BY DR. DERRICK SAMUELS

DEDICATION

To those who have allowed me to stand on their shoulders
for nourishment, growth, and survival.

To those who stand on my shoulders
to see beyond what I can see,
to learn more than I am learning, and
to grow bigger than I am growing.

And

to my family, who unfailingly provide me with an encouraging
atmosphere in which to think, thrust, and thrive.

ACKNOWLEDGEMENTS

The road to greatness is never travelled alone; neither is the path to relevance a lonely journey. This book would have been practically impossible without the encouragement and kind support of many people who have inspired me and those who have allowed me to do the same.

To my wife, Elizabeth, thank you for your love, prayers, and endless support. To our children, Grace and Joshua, you are worth more than gold, and your future is bright and blessed.

To Bill Greenleaf, my talented and meticulous editor, your patience is contagious. You are a man of integrity. Thank you for a job well done.

To Denecia Marshall, who diligently labored to enhance this project with her insights and creativity, I say thank you. You were the first to read through the manuscript, and your feedback made the difference.

Thank you to everyone at CreateSpace Publishing. You are all part of this success story.

CONTENTS

INTRODUCTION

*T*here is something about movement . . .

Imagine how the globe would look if, in the Pacific, Atlantic, Indian, Southern (Antarctic), and Arctic Oceans, water did not flow. Imagine the devastating effect it would have on the Earth and its inhabitants. With all that life throws at the oceans, from the debris of tsunamis to the force of hurricanes, they absorb it all and still flow. If we are to remain fresh, we too must flow.

What has life thrown at you? What hinders your ability to move forward? What holds you back? What clouds your vision? What tethers you to the same spot in life? What discourages you from pursuing your dreams and desires? What takes your attention away from your intentions? What is it? Whatever it *is*, stagnation is not a healthy option. Stagnation is the enemy of freshness.

Water in the kitchen sink stagnates because it lacks mobility. This is one big difference between water in the kitchen sink and water in the oceans. It's also the difference between those who continually strive to add value to their lives and those who refuse the rhythm of change by allowing the challenges that surround them to inhibit their own progress.

Movement is the key to progress. You cannot be a do-nothing person and not experience a recurrent harvest of failures. This is why not to move is to moan, and not to moan is to move. Add more colors to your feathers by applying the force of movement. Give your vision and goals the movement necessary to be achieved. Movement is the only way to remain fully engaged in the pursuit of life.

The era in which we live suggests the essentiality of movement. It suggests the dangers of remaining in one spot with no plan for moving forward. Standing still is not an option. This period in history does not answer to guesswork. It is an era of hyper-competition, such that only the assertive and unique achieve success. It is an era in which the cost of ignorance and laziness is increasingly expensive, and the result takes a heavy toll on its victims. It is an era in which, though many people labor, their take-home pay cannot take them home. It is an age in which problems occur faster than solutions arise.

This is an age of speed characterized by frequent changes in technology, requiring nearly constant training in the use of social media to remain competitive and relevant. It is an era plagued with untold hardship, suffering, poverty, and joblessness, such that only genuine innovators who are willing to be accountable and responsible for the occurrences around them will emerge winners. The hard truth is this: you have no place in this era if you don't have a plan for conscious and continuous self-development.

You need movement.

The purpose of this book is *not* to remind you of how weak and fragile you are, but to reveal the untapped potential inherent within you. Your potential to overcome the problems that surround you is much greater than you realize. Your inner strength, when fully developed, is far more powerful than the challenges that threaten to limit you.

With this book, I aim to:

- help you realize that where you are now is a good enough place to begin anew;
- make you angry enough to overcome the status quo;
- help you think like a champion;
- help you make a solemn vow to implement new ideas, take on challenges, and jump-start your own success;
- drive you out of your comfort zone, the number one enemy of growth and greatness;

- drive you out of the average life, because there is always a level above you, no matter your level of accomplishment;
- challenge you to tap into your innate potential;
- dare you to depart from the ordinary—dare to be different, unique, and customized;
- help you to say "no" to a low-level life; and
- help you avoid choosing the path of least resistance.

You've got to give life the required movement. It takes movement to make progress, and my goal is to inspire you to do just that.

❝ *Dare to be different.*

Dare to be unique.

Dare to be customized.

***Then you will be in demand!* ❞**

The inspiration for this book came from meeting and conquering challenges in my own life. Even as a child, I understood that suffering was an opportunity to learn and grow. Odd jobs, such as farm work and washing cars, developed my integrity and enabled me to purchase books. At one time, I was paid only one cent for five hours of farm work. Can you imagine? But my hard work paid off. I completed my scholastic education and have had—and continue to have—many educational life-experiences, as well. From the time of my childhood, I've always hungered for success.

Growing up, food was scarce in our house—even rice was often too expensive for my family's meager budget. My father valued education above all else. He knew that providing me with an education was the key to giving me everything. My parents sold their bicycle—their only source of transportation—and their black-and-white television to pay for my education. Most holidays were spent studying, sometimes up to twelve hours, rather than feasting.

My parents died a few months after my college graduation. In the aftermath of their untimely deaths, I faced the greatest challenges of my life. I was homeless and sleeping in a friend's church; I left early in the morning before services began and came back only after the last service had ended. I went without food for days at a time; my hair fell out due to lack of nutrition. I was covered with mosquito bites.

Despite these unfortunate circumstances, I willed myself to remain focused. My goal was to continue my education and obtain my master's degree. I achieved that dream and much more. I am living evidence that you can change your life by staying focused on your goals, no matter the challenges life sets before you. Even the chain of poverty and hardship can be broken through dedication to one's dreams.

My scholastic life was far from easy. While in high school, I struggled in mathematics. My father vowed to help me solve this problem and arranged for me to stay with a classmate, Peter Kikeme, who was excellent in math. I lived with Peter, whose home did not have electricity, for six months. During my time there, I digested everything there was to know about mathematics with the help of lantern light. Everywhere Peter went, I followed, soaking up every lesson I could. Thanks to Peter's guidance, I, too, became a master in math, even tutoring others to pay for my college education. Today, I have a degree in engineering and have co-written two books on mathematics. Through focus and determination, what started out as a limitation became one of my greatest assets.

My father was a natural-born leader who inspired thousands. He had heart and never left his village. Leadership without heart is dictatorship. Today, I am a father and a big brother to many. My own leadership skills have helped to create success in others. As a result of my dedication to inspiring others to achieve their dreams, I know seven people—and counting—who now have their PhDs.

Despite the many challenges I've faced in my life, I continue to meet my goals and achieve my dreams. My goal is to inspire and motivate you to do the same.

To those whose potential is in "sleep mode," this book is for you. This book will help you begin the process of rebooting, because whatever is depriving you of the energy to move forward is deterring you from making progress. In the era in which we live, you must compete to win. To win, you must *remain* competitive. When you stop willing things to happen, you stop winning. When you stop winning, you start whining, and when whining sets in, you start waning.

To those who are carelessly awaiting the future, this book is for you. This book is designed to clear away the nonsense, gobbledygook, and mumbo-jumbo that are slowing you down. Why? The stakes are too high to approach life from the wrong angle. The stakes are too high to guess through life. The stakes are too high not to make up your mind to succeed. Success is not accidental. Success is a deliberate act provoked by a purposeful, persistent search for it.

This book will introduce you to the power of optimism in the face of pessimism. This book is about getting you up and doing what is required to attain relevance both to yourself and to society at large. This book is not centered on emotion but on the personal responsibility required to shape, sharpen, straighten, and strengthen your direction of recovery, results, and relevance. Yes, emotions may attract the sympathy of others, but they are not necessarily the panacea for the problems confronting you. I strongly believe that you can create your own desired outcome by taking an oath of excellence that defies failure, thereby consciously positioning yourself to succeed.

One thing I've learned is that retreating into self-pity does not solve life's problems; nor do complaining and finger-pointing make it better. Through my own life's journey, I've proven that by continuously aligning myself with a winning attitude, nurturing positive thinking, employing workable processes, applying tested principles, and surrounding myself with people who matter as I drive toward my desired destination, I can produce results. And so can you.

To those who have been beaten down by disappointment, delay, and denial, this book is for you. In this book, you will discover the need to lean toward a position of strength—a position that stands still when all else fails; a position that cannot be taken away from you when others refuse to cooperate with you. Your ideas, skills, and dreams have been hiding inside of you for too long. The world yearns for your DDD: delivery, development, and demonstration.

To those already pursuing their passions, this book is also for you. You will learn about the dangers and limitations of the "comfort zone" and will be inspired to keep aspiration alive so you don't expire. Once inspired, you must keep riding high. Aspiration actualizes inspiration.

The ingredients in this book were baked in the oven of inspiration and stirred in the kettles of perspiration. This book was inspired by the power of personality, process, people, and principles, and delivered with anticipation so that readers like you can read, respond, and reap the results.

As you read through this book, I urge you to Meditate, Masticate, and Make your dream happen in a meaningful way.

See you at the top!

Dr. Derrick C. Samuels

SECTION I

THE POWER OF PERSONALITY

The difference between those who succeed and those who don't is *attitude*. Those who achieve their dreams have the same eyes as those who don't, but see differently. They have the same ears but hear differently. They have the same legs but walk in a different direction.

There is an attitude that will lead an individual *toward* success, and an attitude that will lead an individual *away* from success. Unfortunately, many today are walking in the opposite direction of their desired success.

There is an attitude for success and an attitude for failure. In life, it takes the right attitude to attain altitude. *Altitude* and *attitude* both have eight characters, but attitude is more powerful than altitude. Just as it takes attitude to *attain* altitude, it takes attitude to *sustain* altitude. Attitude is the foundation that upholds altitude. Without attitude, altitude cannot be achieved, much less sustained.

As powerful as magnets are, if you point the wrong end of a magnet at an object, the magnet will repel it. Your attitude can either attract or repel your dream. The question is: What end of the life-magnet are you pointing toward your aspirations?

Attitudes that Impede Movement

Five common self-defeating attitudes

Don't wish for it. Work for it.

TO LIVE IN A WISHFUL WORLD

There is nothing wrong with wishes. But there is something wrong with wishing without accountability and responsibility; it's like multiplying 100 by zero. There is a difference between a wishing world and a working world. There is also a world of difference between *wishing* things to happen and *willing* things to happen. To wish is to desire, and to will is to be determined to make your wish a reality.

There is a common saying: "If wishes were horses, beggars would ride." To have a big dream in life and not accept the responsibility for its actualization makes you a victim of frustration.

I challenge you to move from a "wishing world" to a "working world."

FALLING AND REFUSING TO GET UP

It is not an unusual thing to fall; there is nothing wrong with falling. We all fall and sometimes come up short. We all have *oops* moments while in pursuit of our dreams. But to fall and refuse to get up is like holding onto your past disappointments, failures, and inadequacies, to the point where they rob you of what's ahead. How can you win if you quit? How can you overcome failure if you refuse to get up when you fall?

PLANTING NOTHING BUT EXPECTING A GREAT HARVEST

Many today wonder why it is not yet harvest time. My question for those people is this: How can you benefit from the harvest without first having partaken in the planting? Those who fail to plant forfeit their harvest. Harvest season awaits those who participate in the planting season. It's as simple as that. Planting precedes the harvest. To expect otherwise is fruitless.

EATING YOUR TOMORROW TODAY

Eating your tomorrow today is like eating the seeds you should be planting. Your tomorrow is the fruit from the seeds you plant today. Your tomorrow requires your investment—an investment of time, hard work, and determination.

Your tomorrow requires discretion. I have a friend who is still paying back the tens of thousands of dollars he borrowed at a high interest rate to pay for his wedding, which took place a few years ago. There is nothing wrong with having the finest wedding in town, treating your spouse to a first-class honeymoon, and buying an expensive ring. What could be wrong with that?

Absolutely nothing. So long as you can afford it.

It is wise to live within your means. Dr. David Oyedepo once said, "Life is in phases and men are in sizes." Wise men think beyond their pockets and live below their pockets.

> **❝ Wise men think beyond their pockets and live below their pockets. ❞**

Eating the seed you should be planting leaves you a victim of want and disrobes you of honor. Many people today are nursing the pains created by the careless choices of yesterday.

We can and should avoid robbing ourselves of the tomorrow we desire. Invest in your future by taking responsibility for your today.

A HEART FULL OF IDEAS AND A
LIFE FULL OF INDOLENCE

What a tragedy to be full of all the things you can do, yet do nothing. It is frustrating to be laden with ideas but languish because you refuse to act on them. It is disheartening to compile more and more new ideas when you have yet to pursue the ones you already have.

As I travel from country to country, motivating people to rediscover the strength in their potential and set goals for themselves, people bombard me all the time with statements like, "I have this great idea . . ."

When I ask these people what they've done about their ideas, they suddenly become short on words. The fact is, you can achieve your goals if you institute a timetable with which to achieve them.

ATTITUDES OF INNOVATORS

Innovators dare to think differently. They do not allow life to box them in. They tear the box open and explore opportunity and possibility through creativity and innovation.

Innovators are not products of happenstance. The inventions we see and hear about today were developed through determination and hard work, not by chance or at the inventor's convenience. Neither can our own desired successes be achieved at our convenience.

Seven attributes of innovators

Let us examine the seven attributes of innovators:

- Innovators are ordinary people who take *extra*ordinary steps.
- Innovators do the impossible with the available.
- Innovators are problem-solvers.
- Innovators are willing to embrace inconvenience in the pursuit of their goals.
- Innovators understand and respect opportunities.
- Time is the pricey currency of innovators.
- Innovators are risk-takers.

What you do and how you do it plays a vital role in transporting yourself from a level of ordinary to a level of *extra*ordinary. There is a thin line between ordinary and extraordinary. This lends credence to a quote by one of the all-time great commanders of words, George Washington Carver: "When you do the common things in life in an uncommon way, you will command the attention of the world."

Extra is not always costly, but it is unique. You cannot go the extra mile in your field of expertise and not be noticed. What is the extra mile you need to create an uncommon life for yourself, for those around you, and for society at large? Your extra mile might be going back to school to obtain the knowledge required to move you forward. It might be your willingness to throw off what has been weighing you down.

This reminds me of a teenager I once taught in a college-level mathematics course. At fifteen years old—a mere high school student—this young man was so grounded in mathematics that he was able to explain the assignments to the college students enrolled in the course.

When I asked him how he came to know mathematics so well at this age, he said, "Professor, I was the worst in math until my parents took away from me what was pulling me down."

"And what was that?" I asked.

He said, "The television that was in my bedroom."

This young boy wasn't the best he could be in mathematics until an object of distraction, in this case the bedroom television set, was out of the way.

I can't know what is in *your* way, what it is exactly that prevents you from being the best you can be. That is for you to determine. But your potential may never be revealed until you identify and get rid of the parasites eating away at your potential: the parasites of procrastination, laziness, excess, lack of purpose, self-pity, unhealthy competition, or dependence on others for survival, when you have the ability to provide for others. Come on, you know what I'm talking about!

Society today is filled with people who ought to be giving rather than begging, producing rather than merely consuming. I challenge you not to waste another day, week, month, or year ignoring what is making you less competitive or less attractive.

You must not die a liability, but an asset.

DOT TO THE RIGHT

In the world of numbers, 0.1 can become 1, 10 can become 100, and 100 can become 1000, simply by moving the decimal point one step further to the right. On the contrary, 1 can become 0.1, 100 can become 10, and 1000 can become 100, simply by moving the decimal point one step further to the left.

- When you dot something to the right, you increase its worth. When you dot something to the left, you decrease its worth.
- Anything that dots you to the left is capable of shrinking your potential.

> **❝ Get rid of whatever it is that dots the decimal points of your potential, ability, excellence, and integrity to the left, because it will always leave you devalued ❞**

Get rid of whatever it is that dots the decimal points of your potential, ability, excellence, and integrity to the left, because it will always leave you devalued. You must "dot right" to reveal and maximize your potential.

INNOVATORS DO THE IMPOSSIBLE WITH THE AVAILABLE

This holds true for many innovators, particularly for William Kamkwamba, a Malawian boy and author of *The Boy Who Harnessed the Wind*. William is a boy with incurable optimism and an incredible story of how the impossible can be made possible with what is available. He generated electricity and running water with materials such as a bicycle dynamo and an electric bell he handpicked from a junkyard.

William Kamkwamba reminds us all that no mountain is too high to climb for people with the heart to solve problems, and no obstacle is too complex for an innovative mind. No more excuses for failing. No more pointing fingers at the government, society, family, or friends. There is no excuse good enough for failure.

Think of GuiGui Zheng, a young girl from China who plays the piano, even though she has no fingers on one hand. Think of Marla Runyan, legally blind, who became a three-time national champion in the women's 5000 meters and won four gold medals at the 1992 Summer Paralympics. What about Nicholas James Vujicic, born in 1982 with a rare disorder that left him with no arms or legs? He graduated from college at the age of twenty-one with a double major in accounting and financial planning and started his own non-profit organization called Life Without Limbs (www.lifewithoutlimbs.org). He went on to become a motivational speaker, author, and husband. Nick Vujicic refused to allow self-pity to keep him down. He reminds us all that the impossible can be achieved with the available.

What you have now is enough to begin anew. No excuse is worth failure. You will not be celebrated by your excuses, but for your results. For too long, you've made excuses for why things are not working out well for you; now start applying principles that will get you back on track again. You have what it takes to succeed because the potential in you is far greater than the problems around you.

Don't watch your potential; work your potential!

66 *Your celebration is in your result,*

not in your explanation. **99**

INNOVATORS ARE PROBLEM-SOLVERS

Innovators of the past, present, and future all share one thing in common: the ability to solve problems.

Problem-solving is a hallmark of innovators such as George Stevenson, the Father of Railways, inventor of the first railroad and steam locomotive; Thomas Edison, the Wizard of Menlo Park, inventor of the electric light bulb and phonograph; John Phillip Holland, developer of the first submarine; and Alexander Graham Bell, inventor of the first practical telephone. Not to mention modern-day innovators such as Jeff Greason of XCOR Aerospace; Jeff Bezos, founder of Amazon.com; and Steve Jobs of Apple Computers, pioneer of the personal computer revolution. The seasoned and successful entrepreneurs of the last century are too numerous to mention.

Friend, it's obvious that problem-solving qualifies you for a reward. None of these inventors chased money. The level of wealth you ultimately command will be determined by the size of the problems you are ready and willing to solve. I challenge you to start looking for problems to solve. I challenge you to stop chasing money and start chasing problem solving. Then, and only then, will you attain more money than you may ever need. Problems in your organization and local community await solutions.

Do you see solutions for the problems around you? Problem solving is your gateway to revealing and maximizing your potential.

INNOVATORS ARE WILLING TO EMBRACE INCONVENIENCE IN THE PURSUIT OF THEIR GOALS

A convenient time to pursue a worthwhile venture may never come. Many waste their skills and potential while waiting for a convenient time to act on their dreams, goals, and aspirations. But innovators understand that there is no convenient time for success.

Many of the inventions and businesses you benefit from today were not born of having waited for the perfect time to create them. Jeff Bezos, the CEO of Amazon.com, wrote the Amazon business plan while traveling from New York to Seattle.

stop waiting for the right time to exercise, eat, play piano

If you wait, you waste.

If everyone waited for a convenient time to act on their dreams, what kind of value would people, organizations, and countries possess? Undeveloped potential is wasted potential. Don't waste your potential; develop it.

INNOVATORS UNDERSTAND AND RESPECT OPPORTUNITIES

No matter how skilled you are, how intelligent or gifted, you need opportunities to demonstrate and showcase your skills, intelligence, and gifts. In other words, your potential is useless without an opportunity to exhibit it. Opportunity gives representation to your potential. Opportunity is the channel through which your talents can be of benefit to you and to others. When you see an opportunity, take hold of it.

❝ *You are useless without the opportunity to display your skills, intelligence, and gifts.* ❞

Opportunity lost could mean success lost, honor lost, and even a future lost. This is why you must understand it, prepare for it, and revere it.

Facts about opportunity lost:

- You lose respect without opportunity.
- You lose recognition without opportunity.
- You lose remembrance without opportunity.
- You lose results without opportunity.
- You lose rewards without opportunity.

UNDERSTANDING THE PLACES OF OPPORTUNITY

You can tap into opportunity

Opportunities answer to location. Social networking, volunteering, conferences, seminars, and workshops are all excellent forums for opportunity.

Some time ago, while in New York, I walked into a networking event where the first person I met said to me, "The reason I came here is to look for people to hire." Interesting, isn't it? Opportunities for jobs and businesses are the hidden gems of those networking events. For those looking for jobs or business opportunities, I challenge you to leave the comfort of your home, join a good social network, and attend their meetings. You will be amazed at the benefits you can derive in a short period of time.

Opportunities can be delayed

Any period of delayed opportunity should be a chance for you to deepen your roots through self-development. This is a time to add more colors to your feathers and discover and develop your talents. It is a time for courage and for focusing on your inner strength.

– that time is now

Opportunities can be created

If you've been searching for an opportunity and can't find one, it might be a sign that it's time to *create* one. Don't underestimate yourself or what you are capable of accomplishing. You have what it takes to create opportunity, both for yourself and for others. You have what it takes to put yourself and others to work. Creativity is locked up inside of you. Find the key and set it free.

Opportunities can be lost

Yes, opportunities can be lost. Opportunities answer to preparedness, research, and development. Think about the many opportunities that have passed you by simply because you weren't ready for them. Opportunity only respects those who seek it. Opportunity only respects those who are ready for it. Just as time will not wait for you, opportunity will not wait for you. When opportunity knocks and you're not ready, she moves on to the next available *ready* person. Opportunity only befriends those who hold her in the highest regard.

Opportunity may not appear in the right uniform

We can identify military personnel and police officers by their uniforms. Unfortunately, many people do not recognize opportunity when they see it. There are certain people who possess a keen eye for opportunity—whether it's wearing the correct uniform or not. These are the people who have the heart to solve problems, meet their own needs, and are willing to create opportunities where, just a moment ago, none existed.

Several years ago, I dressed up like a man going somewhere important. I walked onto the campus of a local college and knocked on the office door of one of the department heads. I had no appointment, but nonetheless was invited in.

When I entered the room, the busy professor kept her eyes on her work. "Yes, can I help you?" she asked distractedly.

"Yes, you can. Professor, I'm so sorry to have barged into your office without an appointment, but I'm looking for problems to solve."

This professor who was so intensely absorbed in her work lifted her head and looked straight into my eyes. "What types of problems do you solve?"

"Math problems," I replied. "And I'm looking for available opportunities to demonstrate my skills."

She then asked, "What topics in math do you know?"

I listed my areas of mathematics study and informed her that I was comfortable teaching all of them. As I was still standing in her office, she emailed the professor in charge of course scheduling, and after furnishing proper documentation of my qualifications, I was in for the following semester.

Imagine if I had merely sat at home watching movies with actors already busy shooting their next movie. Imagine if I had stayed home wallowing in self-pity and pointing fingers as to why things were not going well for me. Imagine if I was at home sleeping when there was an opportunity to be had for a person of my qualifications.

Stop looking for opportunities "in uniform." You are not the only one seeking them. If a ready-made opportunity is hard to find, create one. Look for it. Stop hanging all your hope on ready-made opportunities. Someone once said, "It takes uniqueness to destroy competition." Become unique and destroy the competition.

Don't get me wrong, there's nothing wrong with watching movies, but there is absolutely something wrong with being a spectator during times when you should be in the field performing. There is something wrong with putting in second place what should be in first place. There is something wrong with misplaced priorities.

> **❝ There is something wrong with being a spectator during times when you should be in the field performing. ❞**

Understand that ready-made opportunities may not be available to all people at all times, but opportunities are always available for people willing to create them, for those who seek problems and are willing to solve them.

Opportunity awaits those with the desire to solve problems. This is why you must create an opportunity for yourself if no other exists.

TIME IS THE PRICEY CURRENCY OF INNOVATORS

You can't hold back time. "Tick tock says the clock. What you have to do, do it quick." This was the daily morning song at my elementary school. Many have sung this song in the past and perhaps still sing it today. Unfortunately, few truly understand the impact and implications of the misuse of time.

One fundamental difference between those who succeed and those who do not is in their attitude toward time management. Those who succeed invest their time; those who do not waste it.

I repeat: you can't hold back time. Disrespect for time is disrespect for your own potentially bright future. Disrespect for time is disrespect for opportunity. As the saying goes, "Time and tide waits for no one." Your future is certainly uncertain if you have no respect for time. Time remains the highest currency in existence. Time is higher in value than the U.S. dollar, British pound, Japanese yen, and Chinese renminbi.

Beware of wasting time. Be wary of what eats up your time. Time is your friend, not your enemy. Time is only an enemy to those who waste it. Time is a cherished friend to those who invest it. Time-investment equals wisdom. Time-wasting equals foolishness.

66 Time is a cherished friend to those who invest it. 99

The calendars of those who procrastinate are filled with excuses. "I'll go back to school someday," they say, but they never go. "I'll start that business someday," they say, but they never start that business. They talk the talk, but they do not walk the walk.

66 The line between success and failure is the line of time. 99

Time is where the line is drawn between those who succeed and those who do not. The line between success and failure is the line of time. Time can be lost. Time can work against you. A day misspent is a day wasted. Successful people ensure that every minute counts, that every hour is productive, that every day is accounted for, and that every week is reviewed, reevaluated, and renewed.

Put your brain to work. Put yourself to work.

INNOVATORS ARE RISK-TAKERS

Inside each one of us lies a risk taker. We cannot escape taking risks. Risk taking is not merely an optional course in the school of innovation. It's mandatory. Innovators are risk takers.

Knowingly or unknowingly, we all take risks of varying degrees that chart our path on a daily basis. Those who decide not to take risks place their own success at risk. Those who make conscious decisions to take risks understand that risk-taking is necessary for achieving their goals. Risk-taking is an inescapable phenomenon. We are each fully responsible for the risks we take or fail to take.

To give you a deeper understanding of risk-taking, I have grouped risk-takers into four quadrants:

- Q1: High-value returns + high-risk-takers = *The Place of Champions*
- Q2: Low-value returns + high-risk-takers = *The Fool's Paradise*
- Q3: Low-value returns + low-risk-takers = *The Place of the Majority*
- Q4: High-value returns + low-risk-takers = *The Ideal Place*

we are working on
getting out of here

High-value returns plus High-risk-takers	Low-value returns plus High-risk-takers
Low-value returns plus Low-risk-takers	High-value returns plus Low-risk-takers

Q1: High-value returns plus high-risk-takers – *The Place of Champions*

The high-value plus high-risk quadrant is the quadrant for champions. Champions are high-risk-takers. Champions don't watch things happen, they make things happen. Champions are visionary. Champions take calculated risks. Their goal in life is to stand out from the crowd.

This quadrant is not crowded. It's the zone of:

- creative thinking;
- conscious departure from the ordinary;
- uncommon breakthroughs and success;
- defying all odds to get things done;
- dogged determination that disregards doubtful disposition;
- soaring eagles;
- uniqueness;
- zero tolerance for failure; and
- the inquisitive.

Q2: Low-value returns plus
high-risk-takers – *The Fool's Paradise*

It is risky to operate in ignorance. It is risky to remain uninformed. Not leaning toward the right direction, one that aligns with your desire for growth and distinction is risky. Brushing aside opportunities such as education, training, and research designed to propel you forward in your career and in life, is risky.

This quadrant includes:

- the foolish zone of life;
- the wishing-not-willing-to-work zone;
- the zone of the confused;
- the zone of perpetual procrastinators;
- the zone of lazy people;
- the zone of thinking that everything must be done *for* you;
- the zone of zero times zero;
- the zone of self-pity that keeps you in the pit of life;
- the zone of backwardness, fear, and intimidation; and
- the zone of becoming used to darkness.

Q3: Low-value returns plus
low-risk-takers – *The Place of the Majority*

Many people feel comfortable living in this zone. On the surface, there is nothing wrong with living in this zone, but there are some drawbacks to consider.

Most often, this zone is characterized by:

- taking the path of least resistance;
- settling for the average and mediocre;
- settling but not feeling satisfied; and
- feeling settled but unaccomplished.

Q4: High-value returns
plus low-risk-takers – *The Ideal Place*

This is a hybrid zone. Both champions and the foolish might find a home here, but each come by a different road. Champions arrive here by way of the hard work of self-fulfillment, while the foolish, do-nothing folks *happen* to arrive here by way of daydreaming.

To assume success without creating and following a path to its realization is a big gamble—a precarious situation at best. People don't become successful by mistake. Let me be clear: assumption is not the same thing as hope. While hope leans on substance, assumption is substance-deprived. The road to achievement cannot be found by assumption. Assuming success without making it happen equals frustration. You cannot rule through a cloud of assumption. It is dangerous to leave your future in the hands of luck, lest you wither in ignorance and defeat.

Apply yourself to the laws of success and fire yourself up for the change that points you in the right direction.

66 *The road to achievement cannot be found by assumption.* 99

SECTION II

THE POWER OF PROCESS

The Force of Anger
The Force of Knowledge
The Force of Action
The Force of Confidence
The Force of Positioning
The Force of Vision
The Force of Perspiration
The Force of Discipline
The Force of Focus
The Force of Goal-Setting
The Force of Pressure
The Force of Separation
The Force of Mentorship
The Force of Character
The Force of Humility
The Force of Gratitude
The Force of Decision Making
The Force of Courage

T hinking is a process, and superior value requires process

It takes a premeditated, carefully planned, well-implemented process to convert materials from a raw state to a semi-finished state and ultimately into fully finished products. Manufacturers understand this. Anything of value requires a finely tuned process to effectively and efficiently function.

Just like raw materials go through processes to become more useful, those who design those processes go through their own processes to become productive individuals. Whatever you call them—productive people, innovative minds, creative individuals—these people do not come by these names accidentally. Rather, they are the products of deliberate and conscious exercise, of self-development that evolves through process. Process is a roadmap that can lead you to your desired destination.

PROCESS BEFORE PRACTICE

Understanding process as a means of developing to a level of usefulness is important. Only fools try to bypass the growth process. For instance, here in the U.S., you can't become a doctor without first getting accepted into medical school, studying for years, becoming an intern, and completing a residency. Then, and only then, are you allowed to practice medicine. Failure to go through this process results in ineligibility to practice medicine. Professionals in various fields of expertise—pilots, engineers, nurses, lawyers, teachers—all go through a process of professional development before they are allowed to practice. For example: the mere fact that being a pilot is your dream doesn't allow you to bypass the rigorous training required to fly an airplane.

It takes development to deliver results. Failure to develop through a process that leads you in the right direction renders you a victim of life's obstacles. Don't sidestep obstacles. Do not ignore the difficult or inconvenient parts of the process, lest you be forced out of the trajectory of success.

Disrespect for process is:

- disrespect for discovery;
- disrespect for development; and
- disrespect for distinction.

Thinking is not a "guaranteed overnight delivery." Innovators take time to develop their strength. In the words of Maya Angelou: "We delight in the beauty of the butterfly, but rarely admit the changes it has gone through to achieve that beauty." Beauty comes with process. Think about how *messy* your kitchen gets while preparing a meal for invited guests to make *merry*. Before your guests arrive, you clean up the kitchen, set the table with flowers, and ready yourself to serve. Process sometimes gets very *messy* before it delivers the *merry*.

Let us consider various processes: the Force of Anger, the Force of Boldness, the Force of Knowledge, the Force of Information, the Force of Action, the Force of Discipline, the Force of Separation, the Force of Confidence, the Force of Perspiration, the Force of Vision, the Force of Humility, the Force of Pressure, the Force of Inspiration, the Force of Focus, the Force of Goal Setting, the Force of Decision Making, and the Force of Character.

These processes have been carefully crafted to push you from your present place to a pleasant place, to prod you from purposeless living to a purposeful life, and to propel you from the unbaked side of life to the fully baked and ready-to-serve side of life.

Until dough is fully converted into bread, it's not ready to be served. Until your potential is fully baked in the oven of these processes, you are not ready to be sought after. Your ideas, skills, and dreams have remained in the womb for too long. The world now yearns for your DDD: delivery, development, and demonstration. These processes hold the answers to your long-awaited liberation.

66 *Your ideas, skills, and dreams have remained in the womb for too long. The world now yearns for your DDD: delivery, development, and demonstration.* **99**

THE FORCE OF ANGER

I want you to be angry! Not at others, but at yourself for remaining in place year after year, for not daring to do things differently. Be angry at your procrastination. Be angry at your lack of time-management. Be angry at your laziness.

My friend, the force of anger will prompt your desire to change.

William Kamkwamba, the Malawian boy who harnessed the wind, possessed this kind of anger. When his community was rife with famine, had no water for irrigation, and the cattle and crops were dying, Kamkwamba became angry. Not at his parents, friends, or the government, but against the deplorable state of things. According to Kamkwamba, "It was a future I could not accept."

This is the kind of anger I'm talking about:

- Anger that provokes movement
- Anger that reroutes you from a deplorable life to a desirable life, one of value and relevance
- Anger that awakens your potential and capabilities
- Anger that does not allow you to get used to deficiency
- Anger that does not allow you to get used to defeatism
- Anger that does not allow you to settle for an average life

This is the kind of anger that comes from a realization that where you are is a good enough place to begin anew. It comes from deep self-reflection. You cannot acquire this kind of self-revolutionary anger until you stop pointing fingers at everything and everybody else but you. The realization that where you are is *not* good enough is the beginning of your own self-revolution.

Some thoughts on self-revolution:

- When self-revolution is in place, it provokes the force of anger.
- When the force of anger is in place against standing still, it provokes thinking.
- When the right thinking is in place, it provokes planning.
- When the force of planning is in place, it provokes action.
- When the force of action is in place, it creates the desired change.
- When the desired change is in place, it creates satisfaction and generates energy for continued success.

❝ The realization that where you are is not good enough is the beginning of self-revolution. When self-revolution is in place, it provokes the force of anger. When the force of anger is in place against standing still, it provokes thinking. When the right thinking is in place, it provokes planning. When the force of planning is in place, it provokes action. When the force of action is in place, it creates the desired change, and when the desired change is in place, it

creates satisfaction and generates energy for continued success. **"**

THE FORCE OF KNOWLEDGE

Go for knowledge. It is transformational!

If knowledge weren't powerful, why would organizations across the globe spend millions of dollars on training and hiring experts? If knowledge weren't relevant, why would schools exist? If knowledge was a do-without, why would people be willing to pay constantly rising tuition fees? If knowledge weren't a treasure, why would people crave it so much?

The more informed you are, the more knowledgeable you become. The more knowledgeable you are, the more enlightened you become. The more enlightened you are, the more relevant you become—both to yourself and society. Knowledge, when correctly applied, enlightens, empowers, and propels you to relevance.

Acquiring knowledge and arming yourself with adequate information in your field of expertise is like standing under a cloud as it's filling with moisture. Develop and maintain your knowledge and information base to the point where success has no choice but to rain down on you and your business.

Strive toward a point in your knowledge and information base where your talents refuse to be intimidated, hidden, or doubted. Develop yourself to the point where your desire transforms from a dream to a working knowledge in your area of expertise. This is how to realize your dream, and this is the point where the "rain of success" falls freely and naturally.

Your potential lies at the feet of knowledge. You don't wish for it, you pay for it. Knowledge is a cash-and-carry transaction. Pay the price for knowledge, and cash in the goods contained within it.

66 *Knowledge is a cash-and-carry transaction.* 99

Be hungry for knowledge

Don't be defined by your ignorance. In most cases, lack of progress is at the root of ignorance. The only way to starve ignorance, silence opposition, and make your mark is to continuously feed your knowledge base. You cannot operate beyond what you know. What you don't know keeps you in the dark and limits your performance. Innovators understand this and are therefore eternally hungry for knowledge.

Knowledge in your area of expertise increases your capacity to think on your feet and your ability to make informed decisions. Informed decisions are a product of knowledge. To be deficient in knowledge is to be vulnerable to failure, frustration, and fatigue on the journey to relevance.

Feed your knowledge base by:

- reading materials that synchronize with your vision, purpose, and goals in life;
- attending conferences, seminars, and workshops that hold relevance to your vision, and that help to improve your capacity to function in your field;
- joining professional groups that speak to your needs and aspirations;
- building your knowledge repository by purchasing relevant materials, digging deep, and searching for what moves you, your ideas, and products or services forward;
- being ready and willing to learn from those ahead of you and from those you are ahead of—true leaders are lifelong learners; and
- creating a conducive learning environment that fosters your capacity to think, thrust, and thrive.

I believe your area of expertise is tutoring students with learning differences.

> ❝ *The only way to starve ignorance is to continuously feed your knowledge base.* ❞

THE FORCE OF ACTION

"An object at rest will remain at rest until an outside force acts upon it."

Sir Isaac Newton

Isaac Newton was correct yesterday, today, and will be correct again tomorrow. Desires do not fulfill themselves. Potential does not reveal itself. Nothing moves without a mover. Vision fades without adequate action to bring it forth. Action is the key ingredient to the manifestation of desire. In the school of success, action is the last course you must pass to actualize your vision. It takes action to fulfill dreams.

It is tragic to plan without action. Plans without action culminate in frustration. It is disheartening that people express what they want to become, day after day, year after year, decade after decade, without ever doing anything about it. What purpose does vision serve if never pursued? What is the purpose of creating a plan without the force of action in place?

> ❝ Vision – action = daydreaming ❞

Make your vision happen. You've remained nestled in the hand of luck for far too long. It's time to take your desire out of the hand of luck and take the steps necessary to fulfill your dream. You cannot walk carelessly into greatness. Step-taking is a regular habit of successful people.

Your vision demands the right attitude: action. The force of action is the force of movement. It is the force that shortens the distance between your longings and their fulfillment. The pursuit of nothing results in nothing. When you stop taking steps in life, you stop getting results. Results are the product of action.

A plan without action is simply a wish. Don't die wishing. Don't become a liability to yourself and those around you. Put the force of action in place and work toward your desires.

I challenge you to bail yourself out of complacency and frustration; bail yourself out of laziness and procrastination; bail yourself out of failure and discouragement; bail yourself out of standing still in life without accountability and progress. Things are moving fast in this generation. As a result, you are not permitted to stand still, lest you be trampled, become unnecessary, or render yourself unable to compete.

Until the force of action is applied to the dreams you desire, they are not yet yours. Results require action. Action is the connection between you and your dream. Delayed action causes delayed results, and could even cause denial of results. The action that will deliver you the ultimate result is in your hands. Take that action now and see the positive changes that spring up around you.

THE FORCE OF CONFIDENCE

You have no future without confidence; your colorful future lies in the confidence with which you carry yourself. Family, friends, business associates, and colleagues will not take you seriously until they see confidence at work in you. You are handicapped in the pursuit of anything of value without the force of confidence working for you. Anyone who succeeds is doing so on a platform of confidence.

Confidence is not the same as aggression. You can be aggressive in the pursuit of your dream and still lack confidence. Confidence thrives in the atmosphere of knowledge. Confidence grows in the atmosphere of robust information. The more informed you become in your field of expertise, the more confidence you will display at your work.

Some facts about confidence:

- Confidence is a requirement in the pursuit of vision.
- Confidence is the ability to showcase your intelligence, skills, and expertise.
- Confidence is inner strength activated by adequate knowledge.
- Confidence reveals your potential.

The confident individual does not go unnoticed. The best in you is waiting for the manifestation of your confidence. The potential in you is yearning for expression. It takes confidence to actualize dreams and desires.

How you can build confidence that creates results:

- Live a purposeful life; a life without purpose erodes confidence. Vision is the foundation of confidence.
- Sharpen your skills, grow, and **keep** growing your potential; there is no end to learning.
- Apply the force of mentorship: stand on the shoulders of those you admire to see and fulfill the dreams you desire.
- Watch the company you keep. The company you keep can diminish or increase your confidence; people tend to reflect the company they keep.
- Believe in yourself and your capabilities. Believe in yourself in the morning, afternoon, and evening. Believe in yourself even when others have given up on you. You can't doubt your way to the top.

Why must I reiterate the important role of confidence?

- There will always be things that challenge your potential.
- There will always be barriers that rise up between you and your dreams.
- There will always be obstacles that threaten to deter you from believing in yourself.

Several years ago, during my undergraduate days, I bumped into a friend on a sunny afternoon. Having not seen this friend in a long time, I was expecting a warm welcome, but to my surprise, this was not the case.

Instead, my friend said to me, "While we were in school, you told everyone you were going to be successful in life, but from the stories I've heard from our classmates, it appears you are not doing well at all." At that, my old friend burst into laughter.

Surprised, I watched this fellow mock me for a few moments before having the good sense to walk away.

How can you mock a building that is still under construction? Do you know how beautiful the building is going to look when it's completed?

People can say whatever they want about you. Give them the room to do that. But do not give yourself the room to mock yourself. What you think about yourself, your abilities, and your potential is far more important than what your colleagues, friends, and even family members think. Make sure you are steering the wheel of your own progress. If you cannot fly, run. If you cannot run, walk. If you cannot walk, crawl—so long as you keep moving forward.

If no other animal stands still in this life, tell me why you should stand still and do nothing about your desires. What is deprived of movement is deprived of progress.

Forbid yourself:

- to stand still;
- to be pitied;
- to be lazy;
- to disrespect time;
- to disrespect opportunity;
- to disrespect your potential; and
- to belittle yourself.

There is a world of difference between other people doubting you and you doubting yourself. Giving people the room to doubt you does not mean you should leave room to doubt yourself. If there are goals to set, set them. If there is a vision to pursue, pursue it. If there is a job to do, do it. Nobody will do you greater good than yourself.

You matter!

> ❝ *Nobody will do you greater good*
>
> *than yourself.*
>
> *You matter!* ❞

Friend, you will inevitably come across people in your life who wish to tear you down. These people will exhaust you through gossip, laugh at your work, and mock your failures. They will do their best to drain the best in you. While their full-time job seems designed to impact you negatively, your full-time job should be to positively encourage and motivate yourself, keep your eyes on the goal, and take responsibility for accomplishing your goals.

THE FORCE OF POSITIONING

Position yourself for success!

Positioning yourself for greatness is a do-it-yourself exercise. Exercise your intelligence, ideas, plans, and desires. Position yourself for relevance. You have relied on other people long enough; others cannot do these things for you. Stop basking in the euphoria of empty promises from friends, family, and your government. Board the flight of initiative. Step aboard the ship of action. Climb aboard the train headed to your desired destination. Step up into the bus driven by your vision, and walk the path of productivity.

The smartest "being" I've ever read about or seen is the moon. Why? Scientists discovered long ago that the moon does not reflect light on its own. Rather, the moon aligns itself with the sun and reflects the sun's light onto the earth. This is wisdom. This is intelligence at work. I challenge you to be as smart as the moon.

> **❝ Board the flight of initiative. Step aboard the ship of action. Climb aboard the train headed to your desired destination. Step up into the bus driven by your vision, and walk the path of productivity. ❞**

CHANNELS OF CONNECTIONS

In the face of evolving technology, opportunities for networking have increased and, as a result, are a lot easier to come by.

To make the most of networking opportunities, you must position yourself via social channels; mentoring; creativity and innovation; and continuous self-development. You must position yourself to be located near those who need your product or service. You must position yourself for an impactful life.

To position yourself effectively is to package yourself attractively. We are drawn to those items in the store that are packaged in an eye-catching way. A product without attractive packaging is passed over, or worse, not seen at all. You cannot present your skills effectively without an attractive package. Your attraction is traceable to your packaging. Those who make the most of their skills—whatever their field of expertise—have learned to present themselves effectively through attractive packaging.

This is why you are doing PW. Your MCAT

> **❝ Your attraction is traceable** *perf + tutoring* **to your packaging. ❞** *is only as strong as you are.*
> *#Show up*

Package yourself for excellence, utilization, and success. Your superiority is in your uniqueness, and your uniqueness is in your packaging.

Package yourself for effectiveness, position yourself in the right aisle, and get ready to be sought after and put to use.

THE FORCE OF VISION

If you can see into your future, you will be inspired to dance. Many are depressed because they simply do not see. You cannot see into your future and live in depression. You cannot have a clear mental picture of your preferred future and stay tied down by your past. True vision always conquers past pain and current problems. True vision will grab you, hold you, and keep you excited.

Many look, but few see. Someone rightly put it this way: "Eyes that look are common. Eyes that see are rare." Your lack of motivation in life is evidenced by your lack of vision. You cannot have vision and remain immobile. Dreaming ends where vision begins.

What is vision?

Vision is:

- a conceivable idea that is larger than your current capacity and much larger than your current resources, but well worth the time and effort spent in nurturing it;
- your ability to see a defined path to your preferable future, and being possessed with the courage to accomplish it;
- the inner eye that sees the outer court of possibility;
- the rare sight that sees solutions in problems, opportunities in difficulties, and fulfillment in needs;
- your unceasing, unyielding, and unconquerable friend who keeps reminding you of what you ought to be;
- the dream-world you have travelled several times via the route of imagination;
- that negative hidden in the dark room of your heart that has yet to be developed into a full-sized photo.

Vision does not allow you to sit in a place of comfort. Vision is so powerful that you become naturally willing to lay down your entire life in its pursuit. Vision is buried in the problems, needs, and opportunities around you. Every problem is a gold mine waiting for someone with the heart to unearth it and proffer solutions.

Characteristics of vision:
True vision is bigger than you

If your dream is not bigger than you, it's not a dream that will outlast you. If your dream is merely all about you—what you can eat, what you can wear, where you can live, etc., you have simply signed on for the average life. Do not reduce your dream to only what you can *get*; expand your dream to what you can *give*. Only in this way will your legacy outlast you.

This vision I'm talking about is larger than the self.

> **❝ If your dream is not bigger than you, it's not a dream that will outlast you. ❞**

Vision is the enduring source of motivation

Vision is the source of motivation. You cannot be motivated by things that don't interest you. Your motivation is tied to what inspires you. What inspires you is a clue to where your passion lies. Where your passion lies is a clue to what you should be pursuing.

> **❝ Vision is the source of motivation. You cannot be motivated by things that don't**

interest you.Your motivation is tied to what inspires you. What inspires you is a clue to where your passion lies. Where your passion lies is a clue to what you should be pursuing. 〞

You can't hold back a person of vision

A person with vision is a force; it is not possible to hold back a person with vision. A person with vision is a person of persistent courage. When boxed in, a person with vision springs up in another place. When trapped inside a junkyard, a person with vision picks up the first available item and does the impossible with it. When hit with the stones of criticism, a person with vision uses those stones to build something.

While others are losing ground, a person of vision is gaining ground. A person of vision matters.

Vision focuses your view

Vision prevents you from becoming a "Jack of all trades and master of none." Though the world is changing, and multiple professions can now be managed by one person, this does not necessarily mean you can function effectively while maintaining a variety of careers. For example, it's not possible to be a medical doctor, lawyer, banker, and engineer at the same time. You can't be everywhere doing everything and not become a victim of fatigue.

Vision is the foundation for greatness

Somewhere in the mind of each individual, there is a yearning to become someone of importance, to do something of value. Although innovators understand that there is a price to be paid in getting there, they do what it takes to brave the road to greatness. They are among the few who stand out.

Yes, greatness comes with a price. It comes with the price of hard work aimed in the right direction. Nothing of value comes easy; there is no simple path to greatness. If attaining greatness was easy, everybody would be great. But that is not the case. You cannot carelessly work toward greatness. The journey to greatness is a conscious journey, one of determination, discipline, and perseverance. It's a journey of more push-backs than push-ups, of never whining and never quitting. It's a journey of problem-solving, adding value, and helping others.

Every building must first have a foundation. Builders understand that the stronger the foundation, the sturdier the building. The greatest mistake you can make is to build without a platform. Greatness does not exist in a vacuum. It needs to stand on something concrete. Greatness must be built upon a firm foundation. Every great person we hear of today operates on a solid foundation. The foundation might be the ugliest part of a building—the unseen slab buried in the dirt—yet it is indispensable. The foundation shoulders the weight and withstands the stress of the building itself.

The foundation of greatness is vision. Vision is the path to discovering your potential, and the surest route to greatness. Often, your inner gifts reveal the vision for your life, and the manifestation of your natural talent defines your vision. Vision is not a myth, nor guesswork, but a tangible force locked up within you—a tangible force revealed only by undeniable passion.

What are you passionate about?

Enduring passion is often the catalyst for what is worth pursuing. Whatever you're passionate about may very well pave the path for creating your own wealth. Your passion keeps you motivated. The question is: Where is your passion driving you? Is your passion value-driven? Is your passion purpose-driven? Indeed, passion is a driver. How much trust do you have in your driver? Do you even trust what is driving you?

Passion is powerful, so much so that you need to examine your passion carefully. Here is why: passion is your identity. People associate you with what you are passionate about.

Passion paves the way to self and business revolutions. This is why we should know the story of Foday Melvin Kamara of Sierra Leone. With less than a hundred dollars, saved while he was still a student, Kamara started a business in Freetown that today is worth over a million dollars. With his expertise, Kamara turns old car parts into agro-processing equipment that manufactures rice-milling machines, palm-nut crackers, palm-oil processing plants, and fruit-juice-making equipment. He does the impossible with the available, and in doing so converts waste into wealth. His inspiration stems from his passion for mechanical things.

You cannot hide the person of excellence inside you indefinitely. Excellence reveals itself only when you nurture and act upon your passion. When passion meets action, it often generates explosive results.

THE FORCE OF PERSPIRATION

"Perspire to acquire your desire which you admire.
Do not retire, but re-fire, in order to acquire
your desire which you perspire for."

Seyi Odufejo

This is the force of hard work and moving forward despite all odds. This is the force of "dogged determination that disregards doubtful disposition." This is the force of tireless commitment to worthwhile goals.

Inspiration is meaningless without the force of perspiration. This is why the patriarch of innovation, Thomas Edison, said, "Genius is one percent inspiration and ninety-nine percent perspiration." Inspiration is not a substitute for perspiration in the pursuit of dreams and goals. Not to perspire is to expire, and not to expire is to perspire.

The women and men of amateur and professional sports, including track and field, boxing, basketball, soccer, football, and gymnastics, have one thing in common: perspiration. They practice for hours a day, weeks and months on end, year upon year, preparing for competition. Success has never been cheap. Athletes are driven by inspiration, but inspiration is not a substitute for sweating it out.

Don't be a victim of inspiration without perspiration. Don't be a victim of having ideas but never sweating them out. If you wish to inspire, you must perspire. There is no secret code of successful people, other than perspiration drawn out by inspiration. Give your inspiration the perspiration it requires, because inspiration without perspiration equals frustration.

The reward of inspiration is buried in the labor of perspiration. Go forth and sweat it out!

66 *The reward of inspiration is buried in the labor of perspiration.* 99

THE FORCE OF DISCIPLINE

> "Discipline is the soul of an army. It makes small numbers formidable; procures success to the weak and esteem to all."
>
> George Washington

No wonder George Washington, the first president of the United States, had successes that well outlasted his life. His words reveal his recipe for success. Someone said, "The secret of men is in their story." Reading the biography of George Washington, you cannot help but appreciate the exemplification of a disciplined life.

Friend, you cannot go wrong with discipline. You cannot fail with discipline. I would rather endure the pain of discipline than suffer the pain of regret. Show me a man who is disciplined in the morning of his life, and I'll show you a man who is happy in his midday life. Show me a man who is happy in his midday life, and I'll show you a man who is not toiling in regret in his evening life.

Three truths about discipline:

- Discipline is the driving force of success.
- Discipline is the engine oil of innovators.
- Discipline is the main ingredient in accomplishment.

Imagine how much you would accomplish in life if you were disciplined enough to give yourself the necessary push toward your dreams and goals. Imagine how much your grades would improve if you were disciplined in your studies. Imagine how much success you could have in the world of business if you paid the price of discipline. Success is a far-off dream without the application of discipline. Success will not come within your reach if the force of discipline is not in place.

❝ Success rides on the wings of discipline, courage, and persistence. ❞

Success is no accident. It requires a structured approach, backed by discipline, action, and courage. Discipline is the price you pay for success. Unsuccessful people, in most cases, practice discipline *occasionally*. Successful people, in most cases, practice discipline *consistently*. Success rides on the wings of discipline, courage, and persistence. Distinction in your field of expertise comes through unceasing discipline.

How can you become disciplined? Dr. Myles Munroe said, "Where purpose is not known, abuse is inevitable." People become disciplined when they discover a purpose that is worth caring about and pursuing at all costs.

THE FORCE OF FOCUS

This is the force that matters most. It is the force against distraction. It is the force that places your priority to work toward your dream above the pull of inertia. An inability to focus on goals is a fundamental reason so many people fail to fulfill their potential.

Being a jack of all trades and a master of none leaves you vulnerable to failure. Your system is not wired to be everywhere, doing everything at once. Without the force of focus, you will render yourself weary well before your dreams are realized.

Effectiveness and efficiency in your area of expertise demand unwavering focus. Creative thinkers pay attention to details. Excellence demands that you fight distraction. The ability to fight distraction is a common trait in people of vision. It is a lifetime fight, and one well worth sustaining.

Lack of focus is a deviation from the trajectory of success. Success demands attention. Success demands energy channeled in the right direction. Success takes the force of focus.

People who succeed and people who fail often have one thing in common: they're busy. Not everyone who fails is lazy. The paths to both success and failure are energy-sapping. Many people who are busy are simply not effective. Many are simply wasting their energy on the wrong pursuits. Many pursue dreams and aspirations that are of no value to them. For most of these people, the problem is a lack of focus in the right direction. There is a vast difference between being busy and being effective.

Mike Murdock once said, "Successful people do *always* what unsuccessful people do *occasionally*." Indeed, successful people have learned how to focus.

❝ Success demands attention.

Success demands energy channeled in the right direction. ❞

Most people are busy chasing what is less important to them. The purpose of focus is to narrow your attention to specific goals. The force of focus turns your attention from unimportant things and channels it toward what is imperative in accomplishing your goals.

Are you a busy bee in the hive without any honey to show for it? Is your lack of focus costing you dearly? Is your lack of focus diverting you from achieving your goals? Are you frustrated because of things you've tried that didn't work out? Then it's time to think your life through, refocus, reprioritize, and retool, lest you descend into sinking mode. Stop working so hard at failing; start working hard toward succeeding. Find a pursuit worth your time and put the force of focus in place to harness it.

> **❝ The force of focus turns your attention from unimportant things and channels it toward what is imperative in accomplishing your goals. ❞**

As you pursue your dreams, your relevancy, and those things that add value to your life and the lives of others, you will be tested in numerous ways. If you are not mindful of your goals, you will fall victim to becoming a jack of all trades and a master of none. Do not underestimate the challenges in this life.

Your dreams in life will no doubt face:

- trials that come up with little or no warning;
- tests;
- temptations;
- twisting by the opposition—it is your responsibility to ensure your vision survives;
- the fire of criticism;

- the fire of characterization; and
- the fire of life's challenges.

Lack of focus is the greatest enemy of productivity. Lack of focus will negatively affect a productive mind. Set your eyes in the right direction and take action.

THE FORCE OF GOAL-SETTING

Do not live a single day without a goal right in front of you. Careless living is at the root of unrealized dreams. Your motivation in life is traceable to the goal directly in front of you. Your motivation is goal driven.

> **66 Your motivation is goal driven. 99**

Setting realistic/ too many goals is a diff. topic.

A day without a goal equals a day without motivation. A day without motivation is a day lost. If you keep losing days, days will graduate into weeks, weeks into months, months into years, and years into decades. This is why so many people cannot account for decades spent with their very lives. What a devastating tragedy we can all avoid by setting achievable goals.

Beware: your energy can expire when a goal is accomplished. Life becomes a burden of frustration when there is nothing worth caring about. Imagine a soccer field without the goal posts—a vast, empty field with no way to determine when goals are met. Without a specific goal to strive for, what then would be the yardstick to measure your success? What would you be competing for?

I have always said, though this has not been scientifically proven, that strategic goals destroy hypertension and anxiety. Your strategic goal is your long-term goal. The question is: Do you have a strategic goal in place? Having a long-term goal is good, but not always good enough, because, like I said earlier, goals do not fulfill themselves. A long-term goal requires a mover to move it from an undesirable position to a desirable one.

The route to fulfilling long-term (strategic) goals begins with establishing guiding-principle (tactical) goals around your day-to-day (operational) goals. Having a long-term goal without a course of action employed through your daily life is to have a dream that can't possibly come true.

A person without goals is a dangerous person—someone who has working eyes but who cannot see. Why is a goalless person dangerous? Because such a person is a burden to everyone—family, friends, and society at large, but most of all, to him- or herself. Damn.

A person without goals has nothing to compete for, no platform for motivation. Show me someone without goals, and I will show you a person full of frustration, coupled with distraction. A goalless life is a sinking life that will ultimately drown its victims. Create goals for yourself!

Where do you see yourself in the years to come?

Where do you see yourself in five years' time? In ten years? Where you see yourself in the future answers to planning, and planning answers to setting goals. The challenge of goal-setting doesn't come cheap; it takes time and energy.

Let me be clear: setting achievable goals is well worth your time and energy.

Six common mistakes people make in goal-setting

Mistake #1: Failing to write down your goals

Believe it or not, this is the most common mistake people make in goal-setting. It is not enough to set goals in your mind. Write them down on paper and, if possible, place that piece of paper where you will see it often. Goal-setting is a reminder that there is vision to fulfill. As it applies to you, write down your goals on a daily, weekly, monthly, or yearly basis.

Mistake #2: Setting goals that expect too much too soon

The second common mistake we make when setting goals is that we want to achieve a lot in a little time. It's like having your plate filled with hot food and rushing to finish it in seconds. While it would be awesome to achieve many things in a small space of time, this approach can lead to disappointment when we are unable to fulfill our goals in short order. Biting off more than you can chew is enemy number one of goal achievement. Don't choke on your goals by trying to finish a one-year job in a week. Understand that achieving desired goals is a process.

Mistake #3: Expecting goals to fulfill themselves

The third common mistake people make when settings goals is leaving goals to fulfill themselves. Not going to happen, ladies and gentlemen. Goals neither set nor fulfill themselves. Somebody has got to do the work of making sure set goals become accomplished goals. Actualizing your desired goals is movement-driven and empowered by step-taking. Taking action drives your goals in the direction of fulfillment. Setting goals and taking action supplies value to your vision.

Mistake #4: Failing to make informed decisions in setting goals

The fourth common mistake people make when setting goals is failing to obtain the information required to make those goals happen. Information deficiency is a bane to quality goal-setting. Goal-accomplishment is an information-driven exercise. The more information you have about the goals you set, the easier they are to fulfill.

Mistake #5: Failing to reassess goals

The fifth common mistake people make when setting goals is inflexibility. Goals should be reviewed regularly to assess whether they pass the attainability, authenticity, and adaptability test. Things change quickly in this world. We live in an era characterized by frequent changes dictated by the speed of technology, customer loyalty, consumer behavior, cultural diversities, and short-term business cycles. Reassess your goals when necessary.

Mistake #6: Failing to avoid distractions

The sixth common mistake people make when setting goals is that they allow themselves to become distracted, especially when things don't go as planned. Avoid distraction by all means possible.

The importance of goal-setting cannot be overemphasized. The force of setting goals must be in place before the actualization of your dreams can take place. Wrap your goals around your vision. Setting goals and taking steps toward their fulfillment will lead you to the light of vision-accomplishment. Goals are achievable. I challenge you to set goals, keep them in front of you, and get down to work.

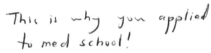

This is why you applied to med school!

(✗) THE FORCE OF PRESSURE

No pressure, no greatness. Every cooked food must pass a fire test. The purpose of a fire test is not to consume the food, but to prepare the food for healthy consumption.

Pressure is not designed to destroy you, but rather, to bolster your attractiveness. Just like so many foods that are unattractive—and unhealthy—when uncooked, so too is an unprepared individual. If you are not willing to pass the pressure test, you are not ready to maximize your potential, make an impact, and be put to use. You become unrefined and unattractive when you shy away from the pressures of life.

> **❝ Stop complaining and start complying with the rules that govern greatness. ❞**

You've probably heard the phrase, "No pain, no gain." The beauty of gold is in its ability to withstand the pressure test. Stop complaining and start complying with the rules that govern greatness.

Organizations are specific in their advertisements for job openings and career opportunities. One common theme you will notice in an overwhelming number of ads is this: *We are looking for a candidate who can work under pressure.* In other words, those who cannot operate in a pressure-filled atmosphere need not apply.

I am the product of an ability to work under pressure. The ability to work productively in a pressure-filled environment brings out the best in you. Fire transforms gold into beautiful jewelry, and just like beautiful gold jewelry, pressure will transform you into a gem.

THE FORCE OF SEPARATION

Separate yourself from:

- the company of gossipers;
- whatever demotivates you; and
- the crowd.

Eagles are champions. Eagles don't fly in flocks. Separate yourself for a cause greater than yourself.

Adopt an on-the-go attitude toward life

This is the type of attitude that leaves no room for discouragement. Whatever has the power to discourage you from chasing your vision is capable of preventing you from achieving your desired success. Understand that it is success that is ahead of you, not failure. What is behind you may be failure and disappointment, but what is ahead of you is triumph. Do not allow your past failures to define you.

An on-the-go attitude is an attitude that does not give up in the face of despair. An on-the-go attitude is an attitude of moving forward even when the odds appear to be stacked against you. An on-the-go attitude looks to past accomplishments for encouragement and tosses aside past failures. Those things that have worked out for you in the past will help to keep you fighting for your dreams.

An on-the-go attitude is an attitude of winners. Winners are those individuals who have consciously deleted the word "quit" from their life's dictionary. An on-the-go attitude is an attitude of getting up quickly after a fall. It's the attitude of pragmatics and optimists. It's a contagious attitude: when it rubs off on the weak, the weak get stronger. When it rubs off on the discouraged, the discouraged get up and move forward. When it rubs off on the disappointed, the disappointed get going and continue looking for the next available appointment.

You may be only a step away from success. Take that step now!

> ❝ **Winners are those individuals who have consciously deleted the word "quit" from their life's dictionary.** ❞

Package yourself for success. Package yourself for excellence. Package yourself for progress. To become somebody important, you've got to look like somebody important. You've cheered on others long enough. When will it be time for others to cheer for you? You've sung songs released by other artists. When will your songs be released? You've watched plenty of movies starring famous actors. When will your movie be released for other people to watch? You've eaten at plenty of restaurants. When will others be eating at your restaurant?

get to eating.

The decision to grow or groan is yours to make. Do you see yourself producing, and not merely consuming? Do you see yourself giving, and not merely taking? You've wished for things to happen for so long. When will you start acting on those wishes? You've planned for too long. When will you start implementing those plans?

What you *do* with your plans and goals defines you. It's what sets you apart from mere dreamers. It's time to think differently. It's time to plan differently. It's time to implement differently.

Success is no accident; it doesn't show up and surprise you. Surprise success is called luck. Most of us are not lucky enough to be awarded success without having worked for it. There is a route to success. Success is a deliberate act prompted by a desperate search for it, and dictated by a conscious effort to separate yourself from all forms of distraction. The route to self-discovery, self-revitalization, and self-rejuvenation is to place yourself on a course that is greater than you. Give what is important to you your utmost attention.

The problem is that too many people wait for a convenient time to succeed. They wait for a convenient time to go back to school, or to get the training and certification necessary to reach the next level in their careers. Too many wait for a convenient time to pursue their goals and dreams. Success is anything but convenient. If you don't want to be inconvenienced, you are not hungry for success.

> **" The route to self-discovery, self-revitalization, and self-rejuvenation is to place yourself on a course that is greater than you. "**

Where you are now is good enough to start
Let me tell a story of two men, one aged forty-five and the other thirty-five. Neither attended school. Both were unhappy with their current lives.

> **" Where you are now is good enough to start and what you have is enough to get started. "**

47

One day, it came into the mind of the forty-five-year-old man to go to school. He shrugged off the naysayers, people who told him, "You're too old" or "You'll never make it." Instead, the man enrolled in an elementary-school program designed for adults.

The thirty-five-year-old man decided he was too old to start school at his age and went about life as usual.

The following chart compares each man's outcome.

Years passed	Mr. X, 45 yrs.	Mr. Y, 35 Yrs.
6 years	Mr. X becomes an elementary school graduate at 51.	Mr. Y, now 41, has done nothing to improve his situation.
12 years	Mr. X graduates from high school at 57.	Mr. Y, now 47, has done nothing to improve his situation.
16 years	Mr. X becomes a college graduate at 61.	Mr. Y, now 51, has done nothing to improve his situation.
18 years	Mr. X earns a master's degree at 63.	Mr. Y, now 53, has done nothing to improve his situation.
22 years	Dr. X earns a doctorate degree age 67.	Mr. Y, 57, has done nothing to improve his situation.

What can be done someday can be done today. Do not let others predict and secure your failure. Navigate your own success. Do not embrace procrastination, and do not permit others to encourage procrastination.

Act now and see how possible it is to become relevant and valuable to yourself and others.

THE FORCE OF MENTORSHIP

> "If I have seen farther than others, it is because
> I was standing on the shoulders of giants."
>
> Sir Isaac Newton

On whose shoulders are you standing? You need a base to stand on as you pursue your goals. You need a source to tap into. You need a path to follow. You need to regularly meet with the people, organizations, and groups that are moving forward in the same direction as you are. You need a mentor. A mentor has the capacity to enhance your potential.

Here are seven reasons why it is imperative to know who your mentors are:

- Your mentor is ahead of you on the path in pursuit of the same or similar goals.
- Your mentor exposes the risks, warning signs, and dangers embedded in your pursuit.
- Your mentor reveals your weaknesses and areas of vulnerability.
- Your mentor straightens and strengthens the path for you.
- Your mentor is your older sibling in the business, who understands the difficulties on the road just ahead of you.
- Through your mentor, success can be duplicated.
- Your mentor provides encouragement for your vision.

Anyone capable of pointing you in the right direction can be a mentor. They may be unrecognized or unpaid mentors, but please respect them. I was lucky enough to recognize my schoolteachers as not just teachers, but mentors. Beyond mentorship, anyone who is genuinely willing to guide or instruct you, who is akin to a father, mother, brother, or sister, can be a mentor.

Several years ago, as a high school teacher, I taught a girl who was easily distracted during class and always late submitting her assignments. One day, I sat her down after class and poured out words of wisdom to her like a father would do for a daughter he truly loved and cared about. At the end of my speech, she said to me, "You are not my father, and you are not capable of instructing me." Wow! What a response.

But guess what? That was the beginning of a positive change in her. It did not seem, on the surface, that my words of wisdom were received or appreciated, but somewhere under the surface, she was encouraged by them. On her graduation day, here came this girl brimming with tears, embracing me before her parents and thanking me for those words. While I did not take credit for the change in her—certainly other teachers had made an impression, as well—it reminded me that words of wisdom and encouragement, when offered from a genuine wish to help someone, can work wonders, and that anyone capable of doing that is like a father, mother, brother, or sister—a mentor.

Growing up, I had many "fathers, mothers, brothers, and sisters." These people took the time to instruct me out of a sincere wish to help me. They guided me and were genuinely interested in seeing me succeed. Many were older than me, but some, interestingly enough, were younger. Among these great mentors was the vice principal at my high school, who also happened to be my chemistry teacher. He was both a mentor and a father figure. Due to his influence, I was able not only to represent my school in regional and state science-quiz contests, but also to teach students from other schools to make a living.

Recognize your mentors, respect them, and reward them equally. Mentors are your gateway to an amazing world of greatness. Go and find the right set of shoulders to stand on.

66 *Mentors are your gateway to an amazing world of greatness.* **99**

The price of mentorship

You can unearth what is buried inside of you via mentorship programs. While some understand the importance and power of having a mentor, many are not willing to pay the price of mentorship. Yes, there is a price to be paid for mentorship. In your case, it might be the price of locating those who inspire you, submitting yourself to learning from your mentor, or paying for the product or services produced or offered by your mentor. Whichever way you look at it, there is a price to pay. But the reward of mentorship, along with your full commitment, far outweighs the price you pay for it. Value comes at a cost. The future you desire comes at a price.

It is not an act of weakness to stand on the shoulders of your mentors. It is not a shameful exercise to search and tap into mentorship programs embedded in the various social interest groups, just as it is not a shame for an unborn child to hook up to its mother through the umbilical cord for growth and survival.

Decades ago, via an entrepreneurship program organized by a local not-for-profit organization in my community, I was assigned to a CEO of one of the Telecom companies. Her responsibility was to teach me how to succeed in business and how to carry myself as a businessman. It was a chance-of-a-lifetime encounter and an unforgettable experience that I take with me in all that I do. There is power in connecting with those ahead of you on the path.

Usually, my goal as a professor at the various colleges where I've been privileged to teach is to see my students beyond the classroom. I see them from the point of view of both a patron and a parent/mentor. I see them as future presidents, CEOs, and entrepreneurs. I see them as the future great men and women of society.

It is my style to motivate my students in determining and developing their inner strengths and abilities, and in discovering what truly inspires them. No matter who they are or where they come from, I believe they've got something inside waiting to be polished and put to work. They've got skills, potential, and someone like me to help them uncover it, cultivate it, and deliver it to the appropriate target audience.

Let me tell you the story of two students I had the opportunity to teach a few years ago. One of them had a deep passion for music. I asked him if there was someone in the music industry that appealed to him. He said yes.

I told my student to search for this person's contact information and email him. I said, "In your email to him, don't come across as a beggar. Just let him know that you admire his music and his dedication. Tell him what you've been doing in your little corner of the world and express your willingness to learn from him."

Nearly two semesters later, I ran into this student on campus, and he hugged me. "Professor Derrick," he said, "it worked, it worked, it worked! The musician I admire got my email and responded favorably."

I felt joy in my heart that I possessed within me the ability to help someone find happiness.

The second student aspired to write a book. I asked him what kind of book he was interested in writing.

"I don't know what title to give to it," he replied. "But I like to advise people on how to make, save, and spend money."

"Awesome!" I told him. "Don't wait until you figure it all out. Write down all the ideas you have already and keep writing them down as they come to you."

Surprisingly, before the end of that same semester, this student informed me that he was writing the last chapter of that book. As the saying goes, where there's a will, there's a way.

Friend, you need a mentor. The journey to your desired destination will be a lot easier with a mentor and/or a mentorship program. Mentors are everywhere. Some are closer than you think, while some might be far away. Wherever you happen to find your mentors, pay the price, learn from them, and do what they do. *Improve* on what they do.

For those who already have a mentor, or mentors, be grateful to those on whose shoulders you stand. You are learning more than you could have without them. Mentorship may be the key to unlocking your potential. Look for those who inspire, motivate, and encourage you in the direction of your dreams.

THE FORCE OF CHARACTER

You cannot carry greatness in a vessel devoid of character and integrity. Of what use is a leaking bucket for holding anything of value? Possessing charisma without character is like pouring something of value into a leaky bucket. Things of value, things that are precious, must be kept safe and secure if they are to be preserved. Things of value require prudence.

As you journey along in the race of life, your character will be tested in the workplace, in relationships, and in social groups.

Character must be tested to ascertain its reliability. Character that has not been tested is unreliable. The question is this: Is your potential draining out of that hole in the bucket because your character lacks integrity?

If so, it's time to repair that leaking bucket. You don't want to pour precious contents into a leaking vessel. Your potential and skill should not be left to seep into the ground under your watch. You must preserve your gifts by maintaining your integrity.

66 *Possessing charisma without having character is like pouring things of value into a leaky bucket.* **99**

Someone once said, "Character is what you do when no one is watching." Character is the ultimate control mechanism of talent and potential. In the following section, I have listed the numerous ways in which we communicate our integrity:

- **Attitude –** Your attitude toward life, and toward others, has a voice and it speaks louder than words. It reflects in your manner and your actions. Attitude is what you communicate whether you're speaking or not. You're always communicating. In a nutshell, attitude is communicated in everything that we say and do.

> **66** *Attitude is communicated in everything that we say and do.* **99**

- **Consideration** – Being considerate of the rights and feelings of others is essential to maintaining integrity. Consideration for others reinforces the golden rule: "Treat others the way you would like to be treated."

- **Empathy** – Having compassion for other people's problems, and expressing a genuine desire to help, says a lot about your personal integrity. Compassion enables you to walk in another's shoes and respond sensitively to that person's needs.

- **Honesty –** If others can consistently rely on you to be upfront and honest, you will come to be regarded as a person of integrity.

- **Respect –** Having respect for yourself, and for others, is key. Regarding and respecting others' opinions begins with having respect for yourself. Until you first respect your own opinions, you will be unable to respect the opinions of others. Respect begins with you.

THE FORCE OF HUMILITY

Many people have been humiliated precisely because they lack or refuse to exercise the inner virtue of *humility*. Many talents and skills never find the light of day due to the absence of humility. Humility is a powerful force. Though hidden in the inner core of most people, it finds expression in our outward activities on a daily basis.

The opposite of humility is arrogance—a force that precedes downward movement. It has often been said that "pride goes before a fall." Pride is a subtle force that creeps into people's lives, eats away at talent, pulls down possibilities, blocks opportunities, and, sadly, has blurred the aspirations and dreams of many. Pride is a force that destroys families, relationships, and businesses. Pride is not your friend. It is enemy number one of progress. Pride is a heavy yoke to carry around one's neck. Avoid pride at all costs.

> **❝ Pride is a subtle force that creeps into people's lives, eats away at talent, pulls down possibilities, blocks opportunities, and, sadly, has blurred the aspirations and dreams of many. ❞**

You cannot hold onto things of great value while standing on a platform of arrogance. You cannot make decisions in an environment polluted with arrogance and pride, without those decisions backfiring on you. Pride leads you to believe that you stand taller than the rest and to see others as hopeless or foolish. Pride distorts vision.

Humility is not a weakness. Humility is strength. Humility is not simply walking down the street with your head bowed. Nor is humility signified by a soft tone of voice, weak actions, or acceptance of defeat.

In my opinion, humility is:

- having it all but retaining the ability to connect with others, whether they've realized their own potential or not;
- having a lot going for you, yet maintaining compassion for those facing difficulties in life;
- having a breakthrough—personal or professional—yet remaining sensitive to others who may be struggling to break even;
- not forgetting the road you walked to get to where you are;
- a secret code to maintaining the height of your potential and fulfillment; and
- helping people to see life, achievement, and success as a privilege, and caring for the less privileged.

THE FORCE OF GRATITUDE

Are you grateful or a great-fool? It's a humorous play on words, of course, but it makes a lot of sense, too. Gratitude translates to being appreciative, not only of where you're at now or tomorrow, but of how you got there. The road you braved to achieve your dreams, and the people who helped you along the way, should never be forgotten simply because you've arrived at your desired destination. As the saying goes, "what you don't appreciate will ultimately depreciate with time."

A simple word of thanks can change the atmosphere around you and positively affect the attitudes of the people around you, be they family, friends, or coworkers. A kind word of appreciation can bring the desired motivation you've long anticipated in your employees, for example. For those times when you forget to communicate your gratitude, a genuine expression of thanks can bring healing to those hurt by your perceived negligence.

I have conquered many of life's hardships, troubles, disagreements, and difficulties by applying the force of gratitude. The force of gratitude is your weapon against stagnation and opposition. It is a weapon of advantage—of strength, not of weakness. If the force of gratitude takes its rightful place in you and in all that you do, you set into motion the reconciling of differences and set a path to peace and progress.

Who doesn't want to be appreciated for a job well done? Who doesn't like to be told "thank you" for having performed a good deed? What employee doesn't want to be acknowledged as part of a team that is moving the organization forward?

> **❝ If the force of gratitude takes its rightful place in you and in all that you do, you set into motion the reconciling of differences and set a path to peace and progress. ❞**

Express gratitude to your team — it does wonders!

Several years ago, a friend of mine ended his relationship with his fiancée because she didn't know how to say a simple word of thanks for the gifts he had given her. This woman lost out on a potentially wonderful relationship because, according to her, she "wasn't brought up or trained to say thank you to anybody." What an unfortunate way to lose out on so much, and all because of empty pride.

There are people who wonder why they should say thank you for an ordinary flower or a gift without much monetary value. You have to understand that not everybody would be thoughtful enough to give a flower or other small, inexpensive gift. It is the *act* of kindness prompted by a thoughtful heart that warrants gratitude, not the gift itself. Every act of kindness committed in a sincere way should be appreciated, irrespective of the gift's size or cost.

You lose out big time when you don't understand and apply the power of gratitude. A man once told me during one of my training sessions that he does not say "thank you" to those under his leadership because he believes it is their responsibility to do what they were hired for.

I said to him, "You're right about your employees being obligated to perform the task for which they were hired, but do you know why you were hired to be their boss?"

He said, "To deliver results."

I replied, "You were hired to create an environment of motivation, and one of the most effective ways of doing that is to acknowledge their efforts and thank them for it." Out of curiosity, I asked, "Where did you learn your theory from?"

"My former boss. The man never said a single word of thanks to anybody."

"And people were happy?" I asked.

He thought for a moment. "Um, kind of."

Finally I said, "Go and remove the 'ums' among those who work for you."

You demotivate, hinder productivity, and negatively impact profitability when you don't recognize, appreciate, and reward those who work for you. What so many managers do not realize is that their accomplishments are made possible by the very workers whose commitment aligns with the organization's objective. Don't bite the hand that feeds you, that bears the burden for seeing your objectives through. You matter, and so do the people around you. The force of gratitude is real and should be present in your day-to-day life.

THE FORCE OF DECISION-MAKING

Every day, every hour, every minute, and every second, nations, organizations, families, and individuals are making decisions. While some decisions offer solutions to simple and complex *everyday* problems, others offer solutions to simple and complex *generational* problems. To be unconscious of the decisions you make is to be ignorant of the impact of your decisions. Without an iota of doubt, most people are where they are today because of decisions they made or failed to make.

At the end of the day, people are the sum total of the decisions they've made, are making, or have failed to make.

The challenge of decision-making

The challenge of decision-making is that you are often bombarded with myriad alternatives. Someone once said, "The hardest thing to learn in life is which bridge to cross and which to burn." That's right. It's hard because of the alternatives. Decision-making has never been easy, be it a nation deciding whether to go to war, an organization deciding the best way to diversify its products or services, a couple deciding whether to marry, or an individual deciding whether to relocate, go back to school, start a business, buy a car, go on vacation, work longer hours to make ends meet, change careers in the midst of economic turmoil, or quit smoking. Quality, informed decision-making does not come easy.

The difference between winners and losers is in the decisions they make. While some have become skillful in making informed decisions, others struggle with the challenge of making quality decisions. The outcomes of bad decisions often hurt. Many are hurting due to the poor decisions they've made.

The power of decision-making

The power of decision lies in making decisions knowingly or unknowingly. A decision is a decision whether it is heralded by trumpets or kept concealed in the deepest part of the mind. A decision *not* to decide is, in itself, a decision. This is a serious topic. I want you to think for a moment about decisions you've made—where you could have been and/or what you could have been if you had made the right decision.

It is amazing that we ensure that much of the food we eat goes through the process of cooking, but we often lack the patience and presence of mind to go through the process of sound decision-making. It is amazing that the gold, diamond, and silver jewelry we wear goes through a rigorous fire process, but we are not always ready and willing to go through a decision-making process.

How long are you going to remain unskilled in decision-making? How long? How long are you going to keep sinking below and not soar beyond? How long?

Knowing the power of decision, and the challenges associated with decision-making, the question is this: How can you become skilled in decision-making? While it may not be the ultimate solution for effective decision-making, the simple decision-making model I've designed for a deeper understanding of how we can all make better decisions—GIVE-IT-YOUR-BEST!—will give you at least a glimpse of what many fail to consider, or fail to remember, during periods of decision-making.

"GIVE-IT-YOUR-BEST!"

Anything of value goes through the testing process. The cars we drive go through vigorous crash-testing to ascertain safety and road worthiness before they are delivered to lots for purchase. The jewelry we wear—gold, diamonds, etc.—go through fire-testing to refine their beauty before they are placed in the store to sell. Students are required to takes tests of assessment before they are allowed to graduate to the next grade. The list goes on and on. Your decisions, too, should be submitted to testing, to assess whether or not they adequately address the need they are designed to meet.

The GIVE-IT-YOUR-BEST! decision-making model will give you, at the very least, a glimpse of how you can make effective and result-oriented decisions. Remember, at the end of the day, you are the decisive decision-maker.

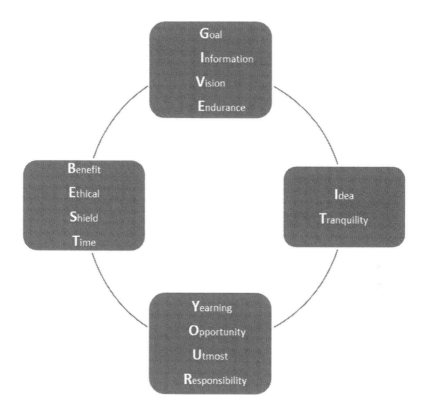

Goal Test

The purpose of the goal test is to define the objective you seek to accomplish. A goalless person will ultimately make faulty mistakes. The energy of the goalless person is spent doing less important things. That is why I said earlier that a goalless individual is a dangerous individual, because a goalless person is a burden to himself, loved ones, and society.

Goals are the litmus test of vision. If you have vision, you must set goals to accomplish that vision. Embedded in goals are choices you must make for your vision's actualization. Goals thrive on vision. While vision is the grandparent of goals, goals are the aunts and uncles of the choices we make. Respect these "grandparents" and "aunts and uncles." They matter to the choices you make.

❝ *Goals thrive on vision. While vision is the grandparent of goals, goals are the aunts and uncles of the choices we make.* **❞**

Information Test

Decisions made without adequate information may leave you disappointed and discouraged. Imagine entering into a business you know nothing about. Is this not one of the many reasons why businesses fail? Research your decisions before you make them. Seek counsel from a trusted source.

Many years ago, a friend of mine asked me for money to start a business. In all honesty, I was willing to support him as much as I could, but he refused to run his desire through an information test—a process of gathering information and testing that information. I asked him, "How can you start a business without doing any research?"

He said, "I already have a good idea, and good ideas sell. All I need is the money to start."

It was then and there that I knew his business was doomed to fail. I told him to first learn the trade, and then ask me for the money.

Yes, good ideas sell, but only when properly harnessed. Starting a new business is a great idea, but only after you've armed yourself with adequate information to run that business profitably. The fact that you are a good cook does not automatically qualify you to manage a restaurant. You still have to learn how to manage resources, choose the right business location, know where to get your goods, etc. The strength of information you acquire determines the quality of the informed decisions you make. Information is your ammunition against making poor choices.

> **❝ Information is your ammunition against making poor choices. ❞**

Vision Test

Vision is the foundation of decision-making. Vision is the ultimate Global Positioning System (GPS) that will steer you in the direction of your strengths. Vision is your seeing power. Remember, you cannot see and not be inspired to take action. Good decisions ride on the wings of vision. Knowing where you're going makes it a lot easier to take the appropriate route. Find where you belong, find your voice, find your strengths, and make decisions that will make your vision a reality.

> **❝ Vision is the ultimate Global Positioning System (GPS) that will steer you in the direction of your strengths. ❞**

Endurance Test

This is a test of patience. Unfortunately, most people fail the test of patience. When people think they can take short cuts to realizing their dreams, they have no respect for the process. Important decisions demand that we take the time to carefully consider all the variables. Making important decisions quickly or carelessly almost surely guarantees a botched decision.

Several years ago, a student of mine walked into my class, very unhappy. By his demeanor, you could easily tell something was not right. I walked up to him during a break and asked if there was anything the matter. His response was: "I fired one of my staff today and, looking back, I should have investigated further, or at least slept on it before making the decision."

Understanding that the decisions you make affect not only you, but also others, underscores the danger of hasty decision-making.

Hasty decisions can affect generations. Some of the problems many encounter in decision-making—at the individual, organizational, or national level—may be traceable to the uncalculated hasty decisions of yesterday.

Give your decisions plenty of calculated thought based on adequate information, and weigh your decisions carefully before you act.

> **66** *Give your decisions plenty of calculated thought based on adequate information, and weigh your decisions carefully before you act.* **99**

Idea Test

Ideas rule the world, but decisions pave the way for their actualization. Ideas draw nourishment from the decisions we make on their behalf. Ideas are the baseline for making decisions. Many decisions have been made based on ideas inspired by people with vision. When we generate ideas through the problems around us, through needs we can meet, and through opportunities we have before us, it takes the right response to turn those ideas into achievable goals.

Problems in our communities, needs that need met, and opportunities around us are simply waiting for our decisions. Ideas are good, but ideas are handicapped without the force of action to implement them. Don't watch your ideas; work your ideas.

❝ Don't watch your ideas; work your ideas. ❞

Tranquility Test

Your sixth sense, or your instinct, is important during the decision-making process. It may not always be accurate, but it is worthy of consideration. I've heard so many people say: "My instincts are telling me not to go that way." Or, "I am not at peace with this decision I'm about to make."

Your sense of peace with any decision, small or large, is important. If the decision you are about to make renders you ill-at-ease for any reason, give that decision further thought and consideration. Many lives have been shattered due to having ignored feelings of unease that arose during the decision-making process. While making decisions, set aside feelings of worry, anxiety, intimidation, inferiority, and unhealthy competition, because you cannot rule or function properly with a distracted mind or in an environment encumbered with confusion. A mind in turmoil is the enemy of good decisions.

❝ If the decision you are about to make renders you ill-at-ease for any reason, give that decision further thought and consideration. ❞

Yearning Test

You can also call the yearning test the hunger test, the passion test, or the desire test. Whatever name you put on it, it takes hunger to beat hunger. If you are hungry enough, you make a decision to look for something to eat. To yearn is to have a strong desire for something. Strong desire is a revelation of your passion. It could be a strong desire for knowledge, to make people laugh, to write books, to educate people on how to solve their marriage or money problems, to nurture creativity, to become an accomplished musician, to offer hospitality, to help developing nations rise above their political instability, or to fight poverty. Whatever your strong desire geared toward helping, healing, honoring, or honing people, it must not be deposited in an unwanted land. When passion becomes your priority, you have knowingly or unknowingly decided the path to tread. I challenge you to monitor your passion and give it the informed decisions required for it to succeed.

Opportunity Test

Opportunity supports decision-making. Most choices we make are traceable to opportunities that have opened up for us. Many pursue their field of interest because they see an opportunity. The challenges we face with today's economy have prompted many people to change careers. Why? Because these people located and seized a better opportunity. Opportunity is the catalyst for decision-making. Tap into an existing opportunity or make one happen.

Utmost Test

The utmost test or what I sometimes call the "priority test," is giving decisions the highest attention they require to succeed. Both success and failure require conscious or unconscious decision-making. Neither of these two factors—success or failure—can be actualized without your attention. Your concentration is needed to succeed just as your concentration is present when you fail; it's your decisions that make the difference. Your utmost is your priority. Desire is not decision. Desire demands your decisions for its implementation. Quality, informed decisions make success probable.

Responsibility Test

Decisions come with responsibility. Your choice will not come to light without accountability. This is a common mistake many people make, time and time again. Once a decision has been made, they believe things should just work themselves out—that success should appear out of nowhere. Your choice demands action. Responsibility is the engine oil of choice. Just like a car without oil is bound to develop major engine problems, so, also, goes decision-making without responsibility. When you lack accountability, you operate below your potential. Making decisions is one thing, actualizing them is quite another. Many people today point fingers at others, things, and various functional systems when, in actuality, they alone have contributed to the reason why things haven't worked out or why things are not going in the right direction for them. The blame game is a pointless sport. Taking responsibility for what happens in your life is the smartest strategy you can adopt. Taking responsibility in actualizing your goals is what adds color to your decisions. Your choice to start a business, for example, may be the right choice, but it is your responsibility to make that choice work.

Don't let accountability for your decisions be an occasional practice. Become accountable for all the decisions you make. Accountability and responsibility are regular habits of successful people.

> **" Accountability and responsibility are regular habits of successful people. "**

Benefit Test

The goal of every decision is to accomplish something worthwhile and ultimately reap the benefits that come with it. At the base of every decision we make is this word "benefit." Another word for benefit is "gain." This is a fundamental reason upon which many people base their decisions. If you can see the benefit behind your decision, you will learn how to make decisions faster. The benefit test always places the value and risk factors into consideration. Benefit is always a deciding factor when it comes to making choices.

Marketers understand the power of letting consumers know what they stand to gain should they choose to purchase their product or service. In most cases, sellers turn off buyers when they cannot adequately explain the benefits of the products and/or services they offer. The benefit test is a pivotal test in making sound choices. The benefit test answers these questions: What do I seek to accomplish? What do I seek to gain? How you benefit from a decision is a fundamental key in making informed, quality decisions.

Benefit is also a motivating factor in realizing your goals. People remain motivated so long as they keep sight of the benefits. Benefit matters in the school of decision-making.

Ethical Test

Decisions should be framed around the principled or moral values that govern your life. Our belief systems dictate the decisions we make. The ethical test answers these questions: Is there virtue in this choice? Is there value in this choice? Will this decision lead to an abuse of power, people, and/or progress? Does it serve a lawful purpose? Is it harmful to the environment?

Shield Test

Protect your choice before anyone else can undermine it. Take care of your choice before someone else does. Your choice is of value and anything of value requires protection. People can talk you out of good choices you're about to make. If your choice is designed to help develop your potential, help others, inspire, or innovate, then it must pass the shield test. Shield your choice from those who demotivate you. Shield your choice from those who want you to fail. Do not let the voices of jealousy, envy, or gossip distract you from defending your choice.

The decisions you make need a valve. A valve is a control mechanism put in place to keep your decisions from deflating. The journey goes smoothly as long as the tires remain inflated. You matter, and so do your choices. Watch out for those who make it their business to distract and/or discourage you, or who deflate your tires of peace, progress, and prosperity.

Time Test

Decisions are often bound by time. For example, you cannot spend the rest of your life trying to decide whether or not you should start your business, go back to school, or quit habits you know inhibit your ability to move forward. Many people have waited too long; decisions not made resulted in dreams unrealized. The ideas, innovation, and vision of these individuals should have found relevance in this world but, sadly, died with their carriers. Don't let this be you!

Timing is important in decision-making. Billions of dollars, millions of people, vast resources of all types have been wasted because somebody somewhere, at some point, acted either too quickly, too late, or not at all. Respect time or be disrespected by time.

" Respect time or be disrespected by time. "

Once a decision passes some or all of the GIVE-IT-YOUR-BEST! test, make your decisions.

THE FORCE OF COURAGE

What if you have applied the forces of anger, boldness, knowledge, information, action, discipline, separation, confidence, perspiration, vision, humility, pressure, inspiration, focus, and goal-setting, and your efforts have still not paid off?

The answer: you need the force of courage.

What if you've been actively applying for jobs but haven't been hired? The voice of courage says, "Apply again." What if you've submitted multiple bids, proposals, and quotes to various places of opportunity but haven't received word back? The voice of courage says, "Reassess your strategy and try again."

What if you studied for your exams but your grades were poor? The voice of courage says, "Prepare for them again."

The force of courage is:

- the force of knowing that others like you have gone through similar or even more difficult situations but did not give up before achieving their goals;

69

- the force that weathers life's challenges and cuts through the fog of setbacks and discouragement;
- the force that reassesses strategies and priorities, especially in the face of multiple attempts to make headway toward a defined path worthy of pursuit;
- the force of taking one more step after many steps have been taken with no progress; and
- the force that compels you to keep on keeping on when you have done all you know to do.

The Pyramid of Courage from the Patriarchs of Courage

Before you give up, remember . . .

Before you become discouraged to the point of giving up, remember the patriarchal father of courage. A man whose life exemplified the true meaning of what it takes to succeed, and became who he was despite challenges that befell him. A man who believed in himself, and behaved like the man he wanted to become until he became that person. A household name who shaped and helped hone the principles of the United States of America: Abraham Lincoln.

Past, present, and future generations will never forget him. The Pyramid of Courage drawn from the life of Abraham Lincoln reveals a man who understood the power of keeping on when all odds are against you. No wonder he said, "Always bear in mind that your own resolution to succeed is more important than any other." This is a statement that reveals the heart of a man who practiced what he said and said exactly what he practiced. What a life! What a journey to greatness! What a lesson to learn! What a legacy of courage!

Looking at the President Lincoln Pyramid of Courage below, as summarized by Ron Kurtus (Founder School for Champions), tell me, what on earth should discourage you?

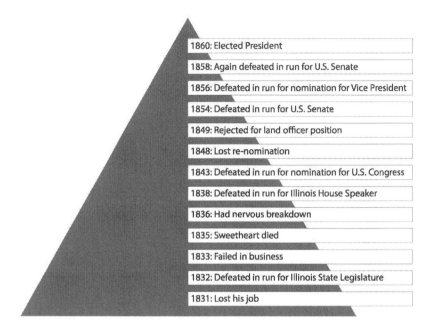

1860: Elected President

1858: Again defeated in run for U.S. Senate

1856: Defeated in run for nomination for Vice President

1854: Defeated in run for U.S. Senate

1849: Rejected for land officer position

1848: Lost re-nomination

1843: Defeated in run for nomination for U.S. Congress

1838: Defeated in run for Illinois House Speaker

1836: Had nervous breakdown

1835: Sweetheart died

1833: Failed in business

1832: Defeated in run for Illinois State Legislature

1831: Lost his job

Before you throw in the towel, remember . . .

Before you give up your dreams to discouragement, remember another patriarch of courage, the living legend of our generation, a revolutionary leader in all spectrums, a man of wit and steel, a freedom fighter against apartheid, and the epitome of courage: Nelson Mandela. In his own words: "I am fundamentally an optimist. Whether that comes from nature or nurture, I cannot say. Part of being optimistic is keeping one's head pointed toward the sun, one's feet moving forward. There were many dark moments when my faith in humanity was sorely tested, but I would not and could not give myself up to despair. That way lies defeat and death."

what is your
Pyramid of
courage ?

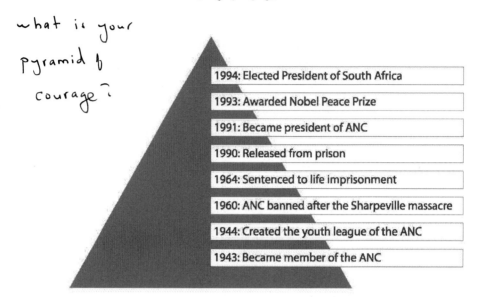

1994: Elected President of South Africa

1993: Awarded Nobel Peace Prize

1991: Became president of ANC

1990: Released from prison

1964: Sentenced to life imprisonment

1960: ANC banned after the Sharpeville massacre

1944: Created the youth league of the ANC

1943: Became member of the ANC

The Pyramid of Courage demonstrated by the life of Nelson Mandela, as shown above, demonstrates a heart that understands the need for *patience* as you tread along the course you believe in. It also demonstrates the power of *peacekeeping* when dealing with those who may not agree with you, the process of *progress* as you battle unfavorable waves in life, and the power of *prosperity* as you focus on solving problems for humanity.

Before you say, "It's over"

Remember Aung San Suu Kyi of Burma, a woman of extraordinary valor, a renowned political prisoner, a testament of courage, and a woman who spent well over a decade under house arrest but refused to give in to the injustices and challenges faced by the Burmese.

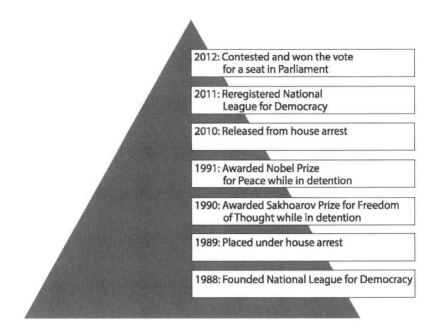

2012: Contested and won the vote for a seat in Parliament

2011: Reregistered National League for Democracy

2010: Released from house arrest

1991: Awarded Nobel Prize for Peace while in detention

1990: Awarded Sakhoarov Prize for Freedom of Thought while in detention

1989: Placed under house arrest

1988: Founded National League for Democracy

There is no doubt in my heart that this great woman of courage understood that the future you believe in is worth fighting for. There is no doubt in my heart that this woman of character understood that the blessing of adhering to your core beliefs, rooted in justice for the people you represent, is more important than the burden of pain surrounding your present moment.

What more can I say . . .

What more can I say? Time will fail me if I try to tell of the man who dedicated himself to the liberation of human beings, a man who fought against injustice and inequality in his generation, a fight which now holds relevance in today's world: Martin Luther King, Jr.

What about the great man of courage, Gani Fawehinmi, who is well known as an advocate for the poor and a man who defends the poor in a court of law without collecting a dime? A man of courage who slept in multiple prisons for saying "no" to the injustices in Nigeria.

When discouragement knocks at your door, remember . . .

- those who endured the pain of the present until all ended well;
- those who did not allow the power of the past to hold them back from reaching out to the future;
- that what is ahead of you is greater and better than what is behind you; and
- that life's challenges will never end, but champions never quit.

LOOK AND LEARN

You cannot learn about the characters of these remarkable individuals and remain unmoved. You cannot explore what these people stood up for and remain in the valley of despondency. They all fought the fight that was much larger than the self. For them, it was about people, and about the pain people bear. It was about problems their people faced. Their very hearts centered on the issues facing mankind.

I challenge you to grow beyond your pain and move past your discouragement. I challenge you to rise above the limits set by your circumstances, to break barriers, to swim harder against the current. Leap over the fence designed to separate you from your dream.

→ *Great idea for a post- share stories f students*

> **❝ Through courage you will emerge the victor, not the victim. ❞**

Through courage you will rise out of the valley of life. Through courage you will emerge the victor, not the victim. Through courage you will succeed and ultimately sing your song of victory.

THE POWER OF
PEOPLE

The Power of People

My biology teacher in high school defined humanity as "the dominant element in the world terrestrial fauna." He went on to state that "the domination they own is largely due to their high biological efficiency and perhaps the catastrophe that befell the reptilian types."

Though I still do not fully understand the catastrophe that "befell the reptilian types," I can relate to the fact that we as humans do possess capability, intelligence, and an aura of greatness. We can achieve in greater capacity what we set our minds to and are committed to achieving.

People are powerful forces. The company you keep matters. People can ruin you or make you reign. Someone once said, "A person can be an asset or a liability. It all depends on how you manage them." We meet people every day. For some, meeting new people creates the beginning of good things in and around them. For others, meeting new people initiates the beginning of a downfall. What a contrast! One thing you cannot avoid is that you will always *see* people, *meet* people, and *need* people.

People are such a powerful force that where you are in life right now may have been determined by people you've met, and perhaps by those you haven't met. Your next level in life might just be determined in the very same way. People you meet can help or hurt you, can move you further up or further down, or may even cause you to maintain the status quo.

JOURNEY OF THE 4 "I'S"

The 4 I's represent four relationship factors that can undercut your ability to be your very best. These are factors you should not only be *aware* of, but *beware* of, so that you can make the best of your life as you pursue your goals and desires.

The 4 I's:

- The Intimidator
- Insulation
- Isolation
- Interdependence

Beware of the Intimidator

The Intimidator is a person who feeds on your fear. He thrives on your ignorance and tries to make you believe that there is nothing good in you. He talks down to you every chance he gets. Unfortunately, this is the kind of person we meet often in the workplace, the family circle, and even among those we call "friends."

Wherever you might encounter them, give intimidators a wide berth. Distance yourself from them as much, and as often, as possible. Separate yourself from the climate of intimidation. Do not yield to their pressure tactics. It is important to *choose* who you spend time with and where you hang out.

An intimidator's entire purpose is to knock the best out of you, to win you over so you can be subject to them. Their intent is to cause you stress and anxiety. Strive to be where you are celebrated, and not where you are merely tolerated.

You are more than *who* or *what* is intimidating you. You must not allow intimidators into your head, or allow an atmosphere of intimidation.

Do not encourage the company of those who:

- make you feel downcast;
- make you deviate from the trajectory of success; and/or
- make you stop dreaming.

Choose your friends carefully. A good friend:

- supports your dream;
- encourages you to dream on;
- looks out for your interests;
- tells you when and where you are off track; and
- is not jealous of your ideas.

Good friends are rare. They are hard to find, so when you find them, treasure and nurture them.

Beware of Insulation

Beware of covering yourself in too much protective padding. Beware of the comfort zone. The purpose of insulation is to give you comfort and protection. If you are going to make maximum impact and leave a mark of value in the sands of history, you must avoid settling into the zone of comfort. Steve Jobs was right when he said, "Don't settle, stay hungry and stay foolish."

The comfort zone can keep you upholding the status quo, the zone of "same ol', same ol'." The comfort zone is the enemy of growth and greatness. The comfort zone can keep you in the selfish zone of life. Life should not be all about you and your family's comfort. There is reward, excitement, and fulfillment in extending your hand to others in need. Don't pad yourself in the comfort zone of life to the point where you lose touch with the less-comfortable things happening around you.

To settle when you ought to be springing forth is to sink, and when sinking sets in, stagnation becomes an unavoidable state of being.

Beware of Interdependence

Many have been disappointed by broken promises—from parents, siblings, government, employees, etc. I hear so many people saying things like, "My uncle said he would lend me the money I need to start my business," or "My government promised me employment after graduation."

But wait. How many of these promises have actually been fulfilled?

Putting your full weight on systems or people to get things done for you is dangerous, disappointing, and discouraging. Don't get me wrong, people do help others to get things done, but your destiny is not in the hands of governmental systems or other people. What you make out of life is in your hands, and you must accept full responsibility for it. It's time to liberate yourself from depending on others to get things done for you. It's time to look inward and tap into your own strength.

Believe in the power of *you* to get things done.

While a few learn good lessons from these types of disappointments, many do not. As a result, their lives continue to revolve around defeat and frustration. The danger of depending on others for help is that it often decreases your credibility and creates an inability to tap into your own potential.

Depending on others can cause you:

- distraction;
- delay;
- demotivation;
- degradation;
- disrespect; and
- disappointment.

Befriend independence. Independence means freedom from waiting and depending on other people or systems to help you when you have what it takes to help yourself. If you sincerely crave financial independence, self-respect, and self-fulfillment, then you must be ready to wake up your potential, sharpen your skills, and put them to use.

Beware of Isolation

Another term for isolation is loneliness. The Merriam-Webster Dictionary defines loneliness as "a state of being without company; cut off from others; not frequented by human beings; sad from being alone; producing a feeling of bleakness or desolation." This type of loneliness is different from the loneliness you feel when you consciously separate yourself for a time to develop your skills or talent, prepare for an exam, or reflect on the state of things around you.

Mother Teresa had this to say: "The most terrible poverty is loneliness and the feeling of being unloved." Myriad experts, including medical doctors, psychologists, certified counselors, and academic researchers, have all said loneliness can lead to increased stress levels, disease, poor decision-making, depression, suicide, altered brain function, alcoholism, and drug abuse. One of the best known philosophers of the twentieth century, Jean-Paul Sartre, said, "If you're lonely when you're alone, you're in bad company."

Therefore, remember to:

- surround yourself with those who believe in you and in your dream; and
- envelop yourself with those whose dreams you believe in.

INFLUENCING YOUR 4 "T'S"

Do not underestimate the power and influence of the people around you. Whom you surround yourself with matters.

Why it's important to know the people influencing your 4 T's:

- They determine the **temperature** around you. Just like temperature determines how cold or how hot something is, the people around you can strengthen or weaken you, motivate or demotivate you.
- They determine the **temptation** around you. Your chances of falling off track can be less or more depending on those who surround you. If you keep the company of negative people, they will create a negative influence around you.

On the other hand, if you keep the company of positive people, they will create a positive influence around you.

- They determine the **tests and trials** around you. Tests and trials are common and do not respect age, color, race, or culture. No matter who you are or where you live, expect tests and trials of various shapes and sizes to come. The people around you determine the severity of the pain you go through during your tests and trials, or the serenity you feel during life's difficult moments.
- They determine the **testimonies** around you. The good news around you is not an accident. At the root of your success are people who have invested their time, talents, and trades in good faith toward you and the cause you are passionate about. In most cases, your testimonies are people-determined.

If the people we associate with are capable of determining temperature, temptations, tests and trials, and the testimonies around us, then we should be more cautious about those we surround ourselves with.

❝ The people around you determine the severity of the pain you go through during your tests and trials, or the serenity you feel during life's difficult moments. ❞

Have the courage to step away from the wrong company. This includes:

- people who cause you to **fail**;
- people who cause you to **falter**;

- people who cause you to *fear*;
- people who cause you to *fall*;
- people who cause you to *forget* your good qualities; and
- people who cause you to *forego* your dreams.

Have the good sense to keep the right company. This includes:

- people who *talk* like champions;
- people who *think* like champions; and
- people who *thrive* like champions.

THE 6 "R" RULES

Rule #1: Respect people

Culture, race, and color may be diverse, and opinions can differ, but all can be respected. Hidden in the heart of each individual is the desire to be respected. Albert Einstein once said, "I speak to everyone in the same way, whether he is the garbage man or the president of the university." Be conscious and cautious of how you treat others. Once again, people matter!

> **66** *Hidden in the heart of each individual is the desire to be respected.* **99**

A very good friend of mine once told me a story of how a person he went to seek help from treated him disrespectfully. Twenty years later, this man asked a favor of my friend. Though the man did not recognize my friend, my friend remembered him. The fact is, in most cases, the disrespectful person forgets, but the disrespected rarely forget.

Respect begins with you. You must respect yourself before others can respect you. Your vision and your goals hold no value if you lack self-respect. Mahatma Gandhi put it this way: "I cannot conceive of a greater loss than the loss of one's self-respect." When you disrespect yourself, you open the door to insult.

Once, while visiting a developing nation, I witnessed a teenaged girl rain torrential insult on a police officer. I was curious to know what had transpired, because a police officer in uniform deserves respect, and seeing him standing there absorbing this girl's wrath spoke volumes. When I questioned her afterward, the young woman told me that the officer had said something inappropriate to her. Looking back at this scenario, I must agree with Fyodor Dostoyevsky when he said, "Only by self-respect will you compel others to respect you." And with Laurence Sterne: "Respect for ourselves guides our morals; respect for others guides our manners."

The point is that you are defenseless when you lack self-respect. When you carry the germ of disrespect, you end up infecting others. When you sow the seeds of disrespect, you may end up reaping the rotten fruit of demotion and desolation. A wise man once said, "Your promotion is tied to the person whose instruction you are willing to follow." For every instance of instruction, there are two choices you will have to make: to obey or disobey it, and to respect or disrespect it. The choice is always yours.

> **❝ When you carry the germ of disrespect, you end up infecting others. ❞**

Rule #2: Reward People

Treat people right. Do what is fair and just, and you will command their respect. Giving people opportunities to be the best they can be is a reward. Genuinely recognizing the people who work with or for you is a reward that keeps them motivated.

Rule #3: Remember people

Don't forget those who stuck by you when others left you in your time of need or adversity. Stay connected to the right people, especially those who believed in you when others gave up on you.

Rule #4: Release people

An ability to see leaders in one's followers, and nurture them until they themselves become great leaders, is a hallmark of effective leaders. What I find disturbing is that not all leaders are able to see beyond themselves to nurture the leadership qualities in others. These leaders, who often feel threatened, are unable to release followers-turned-leaders even after those followers have proven their ability to lead.

Like a mother bird who releases her baby birds after they've completed their "flight training," a true leader is one who sees the value in nurturing another's ability to lead, and allows that new leader to take flight.

> **❝ The price you pay is revealed in the time and commitment you are willing to invest in the relationship. ❞**

You don't own people. You lose when you don't give followers who have found their own voice the opportunity to pursue their dreams and aspirations. Know when to release people who serve under your leadership.

Rule #5: Relate well with people

Good relationships are expensive to maintain; they require constant communication. Anthony Robbins said, "The quality of your life is the quality of your relationships." If you want a quality life, be willing to pay the price for quality relationships. The price you pay is revealed in the time and commitment you are willing to invest in your relationships.

Rule #6: Rebuke people

To rebuke, in the context of this book, means to correct people when they drift or fail to meet your imposed standards. You must do this with respect, and with the expectation of positive change. Rebuking people who do not measure up to expectations at home, in the workplace, in social gatherings, etc. should not make them victims of humiliation. While you cannot condone bad behavior, you should ensure corrective measures geared toward constructive results. Positive outcomes should always be the ultimate purpose for correction.

Six Honey-B's of Rebuke

The lessons of rebuke include the following:

- Rebuke **b**rings out the best in people when properly administered.
- Rebuke **b**rightens the path that is yet to be trod.
- Rebuke **b**eats the bad and ugly out of you.
- Rebuke **b**locks others from repeating the same mistakes; rebuke stifles negative reinforcement.
- Rebuke, when properly applied, **b**uilds people up.
- Rebuke is the **b**oat that keeps you from sinking in the murky water.

The beauty of rebuke or correction cannot be overemphasized. However, remember that although correction does much, encouragement of positive behavior does much more. As you use the rod of rebuke, do not forget to apply the balm of encouragement, lest you leave people worse off than before.

> **66** *As you use the rod of rebuke, do not forget to apply the balm of encouragement, lest you leave people worse off than before.* **99**

THE POWER OF PRINCIPLES

Every person is consciously or unconsciously standing on something. The questions are: What are you standing on? What do you rely on? What do you lean on?

What you stand on, rely on, or lean on can protect or pummel you.

WHAT IS A PRINCIPLE?

The word *principle* means "a rule or code of conduct, a moral value or responsibility that someone has toward a certain subject." However you define *principle*, your principles in life are what define you. Whatever you stand for over a long period of time become the principles you live by and reveal the values you stand on.

Some stand on excuses. These are people who give excuses as to why things aren't working for them. They waste time explaining to all kinds of people their situations—pointing fingers, shifting blame, etc. They blame their unfortunate circumstances on everything and everybody except, of course, themselves.

Others stand on procrastination. These people have perfected the art of procrastination to the point where they do not view their potential as something worth developing. Their talents and skills are seen as toys rather than useful tools in their hands. These are people who pay no respect to time and have no idea that opportunity can be lost. They know they have what it takes to succeed, make a positive mark in their field of expertise, and add value to society, but they choose to postpone, dillydally, hem and haw—you name it—until they've squandered their chance at success and become victims of frustration.

Others stand on everything that passes by. These people do what they see others doing. These are the individuals I refer to as jack of all trades and master of none. They have no priorities of their own. These are people who are constantly chasing pennies, when the real worth in them remains untapped, undeveloped, and underutilized. No wonder Charles Dickens said, "I never could have done what I have done without the habits of punctuality, order, and diligence, without the determination to concentrate myself on one subject at a time."

PRINCIPLE #1: HAVE THE RIGHT KEY HANDY

Life operates on principles. Business success operates on principles. Good and rewarding relationships operate on principles. Good principles, when correctly applied, open doors of opportunity. Principles are keys to greatness. Principles are keys to success. Therefore:

$$Principle = Key$$

It takes the right key to open the right door. No matter how small or gigantic the door, each requires the right key to gain access to the treasure within. In other words, all doors are subject to the right keys, irrespective of their size. The right key will unlock the gate to treasure. When the right key is acquired, a door has no choice but to open for you. Success is therefore key-dependent.

Your access to the next level in life, the next level of comfort, the next level of exploit, and the next level of fulfillment is dependent on the key you have in your hand. You cannot operate the right door with the wrong key and achieve a positive outcome. Wrong principles are like trying to open doors with the wrong keys.

Examine the key in your hand. Is it working for you? If you've been trying for decades to break through in your career with no success, perhaps it's time to check the key you've been using.

It is possible that your struggles, and perhaps the frustrations of yesteryear, are evidence that you're holding onto the wrong key. You cannot stick to losing strategies and be on the winning side of life. Someone once defined madness as "doing the same thing over and over again and expecting different results." How long are you going to hang onto a key that does not unlock the door you wish to open?

The right key is not afraid of big doors, nor is it intimidated by giant gates. What many have termed as insurmountable business difficulties, or as personal challenges, might just be a problem of not having the right key.

The right key = the right principles.

> **❝ The right key is not afraid of big doors, nor is it intimidated by giant gates. ❞**

The danger of holding onto the wrong key is that it keeps you away from accessing desired results. Nothing erodes confidence more than operating with the wrong principles for too long. When you operate by the right principles, you can't help but be bold. Let go of the wrong keys in your hand and reach for the right ones—the ones that open doors of unimaginable productivity and progress.

PRINCIPLE #2: PLACE VALUE ON YOUR POTENTIAL

How do you view your potential? Do you regard your talents and skills as toys or tools? What price tag would you place on your skills—that of a toy or a tool? The value you place on your skills matters. How you see your potential matters. It is impossible to fumble when you see the worth in your potential. The potential in you is a tool, not a toy. Toys belong in the hands of children, while tools belong in the hands of responsible adults. Tools are designed to work for you and help you create wealth.

Are your skills tools or toys?

Children are known to handle toys carelessly, but it is expected of adults to handle tools carefully and cautiously. Children play with toys, while adults work with tools. Are you an adult still hooked on toys? When you have no regard for the tool in your hand, it is no more than a toy in the hand of a child.

Are you an adult or a child?

As an adult, if you treat or handle your skills in the same way a child treats or handles toys, you are no more than a child in an adult uniform. Not knowing the value of things is the beginning of misuse. This explains why so many leaders, especially those in developing nations endowed with natural resources, become corrupt while holding political office; they do not respect the importance of those resources.

Wealth is wasted every second of every day. A wise man once said, "Abuse is absolutely unavoidable if the purpose for its existence is not known." Do you know the purpose of your potential? If you don't know, you're next in line to abuse and squander it.

> **❝ When you have no regard for the tool in your hand, it is no more than a toy in the hand of a child. ❞**

What is that skill you have belittled for too long? What is the purpose of the potential you've been trampling for so long? Maybe you have a knack for connecting with others and influencing situations positively, or an ability to lead or teach. Perhaps you have a natural aptitude for initiating concepts, or designing, or manufacturing and showcasing your own product.

Whatever your skill, you have neglected it for too long. Your tool is right there for the taking. Wake it up, because it is a gift that must not be wasted.

Your gift: Teaching

Tools must be put to use

Tools are of no value until they are put to use. Successful people learn how to put their tools to use, while others leave their tools to rust. There is dignity in putting your skills to work.

How can you elevate your tutoring skills today?

> **❝ Tools are of no value until they are put to use. ❞**

There is self-respect in labor. Putting yourself to good use is a noble course. No wonder Abraham Lincoln once wrote in a letter to his son's teacher, "Teach my son that a dollar earned is worth more than five dollars found."

Take time to:

- sharpen your tools;
- package yourself for success;
- dress for success; and
- sharpen your potential.

Your tools, as mentioned earlier, are your skills for exploiting your relevance, and are heavily tied to your ability to continuously sharpen them. Sharpened tools will make you more marketable and more competitive in the global market. You cannot operate on twentieth-century sense in a twenty-first-century world and expect the same results. As Albert Einstein argued, "We cannot solve our problems with the same thinking we used when we created them."

Many rush into the field too quickly without first sharpening their tools.

First, you must:

- develop inwardly before making your outward presentation; and
- develop privately before your public display begins.

Unsharpened tools wear out quickly. Many have worn themselves out because they mistakenly believed they could use their potential without first undergoing the work of self-development, only to discover that self-development comes before self-display, and that private discipline comes before public display. Sharpen your tools, and you'll get the job done easier and faster.

Learn your trade before attempting to sell your product. You have no business in the public square if you have not first existed in the private place. Some may have to retreat to the private place of self-discovery and self-development before their talents can have a meaningful effect in the public arena. Don't rush out too quickly to display your skills publically. Rather, spend a little more time, if needed, in the private room of learning all the ins and outs of your trade. Then and only then will you be able to command respect, returns, rewards, recovery, and rejuvenation.

Tool usage must be properly understood

Tools come with instructions. Tools can be preserved by adhering to the manufacturer's instructions, and your obedience to those instructions is your guarantee for safety. Simply put, your willingness to heed instruction is your warranty for the longevity and vitality of your potential. Acquire the proper instruction for tapping into your potential for maximum impact.

What you don't understand can result in an accident. Much potential has been wasted, and much more will be wasted, because many people lack full understanding of their usable skills. What you don't understand, in most cases, will be abused. Abuse of potential is a common phenomenon for those who do not have a complete understanding of their skills and how to put them to work. Having potential without a working knowledge of your skills is like leaving the key to your car in the hand of a three-year-old and asking that toddler to drive. What would you expect of a three-year-old driver? Safety? Probably not.

Don't abuse your potential. Find out what it takes to make it valuable. Find out what it takes to showcase your skills.

Tools must be preserved

We preserve food from becoming spoiled, don't we? Tools, too, must be preserved, just like eggs and milk. Spoiled food ends up in the trash. Potential can end up in the trash, too, if not properly preserved.

How can you "refrigerate" your potential to keep it from rotting? Keep your potential up-to-date. Stay informed about current developments in your field of expertise. Update and increase your knowledge base regularly. You cannot thrive in the world of technology, for example, if you don't stay up-to-date with the current trends in that field. Those who don't bother to stay abreast of the latest information quickly become obsolete and irrelevant.

PRINCIPLE #3: SUCCESS IS NEVER CHEAP

If success is not in your heart, do not expect it to be in your hands. Success requires conceptual thinking; success is a mind-thing. Do you have the mind for success? Are you engaging your mind productively? As the saying goes, "The mind is a terrible thing to waste."

A wasted mind is a wasted life.

You cannot succeed until you can visualize yourself capable of succeeding. You cannot make a dent in failure until you see yourself capable of defeating failure. Success is not held in the hands of those who do not have the heart for it.

The trajectory of success

Success has a trajectory. Don't depart from this trajectory. It is the only route to a valuable destination. On a daily basis, many people are drawn away from this trajectory. The trajectory of success is like a magnetic field.

Magnetic fields are known for their direction and strength. A deviation from the trajectory of success is a deviation from the path of strength.

The trajectory of success is the trajectory of:

- being focused in your assignment;
- hard work with the right key;
- willingness to adapt to changes;
- responding rather than reacting to issues; and
- updating your information base to remain relevant.

It's not easy to stay focused. It takes energy, conscious effort, and a determination to fight distractions of all kinds. The danger of distraction is that it comes in various sizes, shapes, and colors. Often, distractions are difficult to detect, especially the little ones. Distraction hides itself in our friends, jobs, desires, to-do lists, societal pressures, and habits. Who or what distracts you from your vision, from achieving your goals?

Distraction causes delay. Distraction takes us away from the magnetic field of success. When you lose sight of the bigger picture, your attention diverts to unimportant things. Don't end up a victim of distraction. Develop a thick skin and use it to shield yourself from distraction. Refuse to be dragged out of the trajectory of success.

66 *When you lose sight of the bigger picture, your attention diverts to unimportant things.* 99

 Be careful of your last success
Don't let your last success be your final success. While it's good to celebrate success and feel gratified by your last achievement, don't allow your accomplishments to keep you from envisioning your next success. Your current success should spur you to the next level.

PRINCIPLE #4: EXPECT CHANGES ALONG THE WAY

Change is a mandatory recipe for progress, and is considered by many researchers and philosophers as the only constant in life. The highly competitive businesses of today have one thing in common: they adapt to change quickly, and manage change effectively and efficiently. On the other hand, businesses that do not embrace change, or are slow to implement change, often find themselves running way behind in the race.

> **66** *Change is a mandatory recipe for progress.* **99**

We live in a fast-paced world dictated by speed and anchored by technology. Take a look at the rate at which technology continually launches into the market, or at how businesses today dictate the frequent changes in technology. Take a look at how technology shortens a product's life-cycle. You cannot afford the luxury of remaining unprepared, unrefined, and uninformed in your field of practice. You shortchange your vision if you don't ride the wings of change; it will send you down the road to becoming irrelevant and obsolete.

Remember: if you fail to update yourself, you will soon be outdated.

PRINCIPLE #5: SEE SACRIFICE BEFORE REWARD

Champions see sacrifice before reward. You are rewarded for the sacrifices you are willing to make. Reward is the end product of sacrifice. In most cases, reward is hidden in the heart of problems, needs, and opportunities. Focus your pursuit on what you can do rather than what you can get.

There are rewards buried in those volunteer services in your communities. Years ago, as a project manager, I asked several members of my team if they would volunteer to supervise the operational level of the project task. Out of the twenty people I posed the request to, only three showed interest—by immediately raising their hands, indicating their willingness to serve. I then shared information about a reward package associated with performing this particular task. Several of the team members initially unwilling to volunteer said something along the lines of "I wish you'd told us there was a reward package involved."

I said to them, "Always see sacrifice before reward. Reward is good, but it takes sacrifice wrapped in responsibility to earn it."

Each year, I look forward to watching CNN Heroes, anchored by Anderson Cooper. The heroes rewarded on the program have these things in common: they sacrificed their time, gave their talents, and tapped into their various resources to help people who, in most cases, have been ignored or relegated to various dark corners around the world. They saw problems and offered a helping hand to make the world a better place.

I will share my story in the next section, titled, "Resolve to leave people better than when you met them." It's a story of how I saw sacrifice before reward during the year I spent in community service.

66 *Always see sacrifice before reward.* 99

PRINCIPLE #6: RESOLVE TO LEAVE PEOPLE BETTER THAN YOU MET THEM

Great people possess the following qualities:

- a conscious resolve to leave people better than when they met them
- a conscious resolve to bring out the best in people
- a conscious resolve to add value to whatever they can, as often as they can

66 *You can achieve what you are consciously passionate about.* 99

You can achieve what you are consciously passionate about. This is the principle for those who understand the power of making a difference in people's lives; this is exactly how true visionaries think.

Several years ago, I served a one-year post to a local government headquarters in a developing nation—similar to what we might call a county. Because there were a number of us serving in the same capacity, the group was posted to a local council area far from our accommodations in town and from the state capital—far from the comforts to which we were all accustomed.

We were each given a primary task to accomplish in the interest of bettering the quality of life for the people living in the area. As taxing as my primary assignment was, I frequently worked beyond my regular duties by assisting people in the local area, making it necessary for me to travel to the various villages around the region. When I saw the deplorable conditions these villagers lived in every day, I made a solemn vow to leave them five times better than when I met them by carrying out five developmental community projects. I titled the project *Five Fingers, Five Projects*.

Project 1:

In one of the villages, I learned that pregnant women were forced to travel on foot, approximately forty kilometers down a dusty road to a town clinic, for prenatal care and to deliver their babies. I was horrified to learn, from several of the villagers, that there had been incidents of pregnant women becoming ill or being harmed on route to the clinic. To this end, I wrote a letter to the then-governor's wife, the Commissioner for Women's Affairs at the State Ministry of Health, stating the need for a health post in this particular village. My efforts paid off.

Once the governor's wife entered the picture, money was raised for the building of an outpost clinic for the community, and a committee was appointed to oversee the funds raised for its construction.

The lesson here is one that supports the true saying, "Where there's a will, there's a way."

Project 2:

My second project was the design and construction of a smokeless oven. In many of the villages, the preparing of cassava flakes was the most common job for women. An extremely arduous and dangerous job, the frying phase often engulfed the women in smoke as they worked.

While researching the process, I learned that the smoke inhalation could cause the decomposition of hemoglobin, increasing the risk of heart attack in these women. Following this discovery, I contacted UNICEF to ask if they would assist with the sponsoring and constructing of smokeless ovens for each of the local villages.

With the help of consultants and resource approval from UNICEF, thirty-eight smokeless ovens were constructed for an initial demonstration, and local volunteers were trained in how to properly use them.

The wisdom here is this: help is available to those willing to seek solutions to problems.

Project 3:

One of the most troubling aspects of village life was the ever-present suffering caused by guinea worm disease (GWD). Due to a lack of access to potable drinking water, many villagers commonly drank from the stagnant, parasite-contaminated water in ponds created by the rainy season, causing widespread disease and discomfort.

Concerned for the well-being of the numerous GWD victims I came to know, I placed a call to the Guinea Worm Disease Eradication Agency established by former U.S. President Jimmy Carter. With the help and sacrifice from the caring and skilled people involved with the organization, filters were provided, and hand-drilled pumps were used to move the water up off the ground.

The lesson here is this: a little extra help to those in need can go a long way in bringing extraordinary relief and comfort.

Project 4:

My fourth project revolved around educating villages about AIDS (Acquired Immune Deficiency Syndrome). Nothing gets done until someone is willing to initiate the process of getting things done. In this project, I contacted the USAID office, which provided important resource materials for each of the villages.

Stop looking at problems, and start solving them.

Project 5:

The final project for Five Fingers, Five Projects was the Pineapple Orchard Farm. The local department of agriculture approved a parcel of land in which I planted 200 pineapple suckers. The usual farmed crops in these communities consisted of cassava, yam, and cocoyam, all of which are rich in carbohydrates. The government's encouragement to farm produce rich in Vitamin C prompted my decision to carry out the pineapple farming project.

I came to this area unrecognized but did not leave unnoticed, particularly by those positively affected by the projects I initiated and carried through. What I was able to accomplish in those small, neglected villages drew the attention of leaders in both local and state government, resulting in the presentation of awards in my honor.

I came, I saw, and I conquered, by leaving the villagers five times better off than when I met them. Your distinction will not come by sitting on the fence.

❝ Solve problems, and you will be remembered. ❞

97

The problems around you are waiting for your solutions.

- Solve problems, and you will find *recognition.*
- Solve problems, and you will reap *rewards.*
- Solve problems, and you will be *remembered.*

PRINCIPLE #7: DO POSITIVE THINGS THAT WILL OUTLAST YOU

The beauty of solutions is that they outlast those who offer them. Thomas Edison offered a solution by creating light in darkness without need of fire or fuel. We still have not forgotten him. Mother Theresa connected with the suffering people, gave comfort, and won the Nobel Peace Prize. She is still remembered today. Steve Jobs created solutions for numerous communications problems and achieved many landmark milestones in the world of technology. The world stood still at his passing.

66 *Recognition lies in the solving of problems.* 99

Don't look for recognition in the wrong place. Recognition lies in the solving of problems. People, communities, and organizations of all kinds are waiting for your solutions to their problems. Do not disappoint them.

PRINCIPLE #8: PARTNER NO MORE WITH PROCRASTINATION

Procrastination is not only a thief of time, but a thief of destiny. Procrastination is a trap that has kept many from achieving their worthwhile goals, a trap that limits people to experiencing life from the constrained safety of their comfort zones. Procrastination is like a raincoat: just as raincoats prevent us from feeling the impact of a cleansing rain, procrastination shields people from achieving success.

> **" Action is in front of you. Procrastination is behind you. "**

If you desire a life of value, I implore you to remove the raincoat of procrastination. Action is in front of you. Procrastination is behind you.

PRINCIPLE #9: DISPLAY YOUR TALENTS

Possessing skills does not automatically equal greatness. Until potential is displayed, it will not be realized in the arena of value. Display your talents to reveal their value.

For example, it takes a product of value to command the respect and attention of customers. I've shopped in stores of all sizes, from Wal-Mart and Macy's to the smaller, locally owned shops in my neighborhood. All stores share one thing in common: they display their goods at all times. The goods are not locked up in a warehouse somewhere.

Many useful skills have been locked up in the warehouses of laziness, reticence, intimidation, shame, distraction, and ignorance for far too long.

Where are your talents locked up? Don't die unfulfilled. Don't die nursing regret. Find the key, open that warehouse, and unlock your talent. Your potential holds no value unless you display it. When you display your skills to your target audience, it increases your chances of finding fulfillment and achieving the desires in your heart.

Begging is more difficult than working

In my travels around the world, I've witnessed many people begging for spare change. Those who are sick or living with disabilities have legitimate reasons for asking for help, and to those people, I do give whenever possible. But, too often, you see people begging who appear to be able-bodied, strong, and vital. The problem with such beggars is that they clearly don't realize that begging is infinitely more difficult than working.

How do I know? Some years ago, I boarded a train on my way to work, only to realize that I'd forgotten my wallet containing my ticket, identification, money, and credit cards. Here I was, well dressed in a suit and tie and polished shoes, and having nothing to show the train conductor who was asking for my ticket. I was so embarrassed, I began to sweat. I had never been in that situation before. I tried to explain, but the train conductor wasn't the least bit interested in my explanation. He wanted my ticket, and that was all.

Mortified, and at a loss for what to do, I glanced around at the other passengers on the train, hoping to find some support from my fellow commuters. To my surprise and relief, another passenger stepped up out of compassion for my circumstances and paid for me.

That single moment of desperation, of having to rely on another person to fix my situation, was enough for me to know that I could never, under any circumstance, ask for a handout when my body and mind were capable of work.

There is a certain group of beggars I greatly admire. I see them often in the subways and on street corners, demonstrating their talent, be it musical or otherwise. In the midst of their predicaments, they never quit trying. These are the people to whom I am always willing to give my "widow's mite." People in this category understand that *the best angle from which to approach a problem is the try-angle.* As a result, they never quit showcasing their gifts or what they are capable of achieving when given the opportunity. I have seen, over and over, different people in various locations around the world using seemingly insignificant materials to show people they've got talent—ranging from plates and cups used as instruments, to clapping and dancing.

Albert Einstein said, "You never fail until you stop trying." This truth is at work in these kinds of people. Ted Williams, the homeless man with the golden radio voice, is one such person. As a panhandler, he displayed his talent and caught the attention of the public and the media, not to mention the Cleveland Cavaliers, who offered him a job. Displaying your talent announces your arrival.

Friend, what you've got is enough if only you appreciate and develop it. The worth of your skills is measured by how much you appreciate them. How much you appreciate your skills reflects in your willingness to display them. It's time to kiss your fear and shyness goodbye. It is time to showcase your talent. Act now, and your story of success could be the next to be shared.

PRINCIPLE #10: DON'T FORGET THERE IS ALWAYS A STREAM BEFORE YOUR DREAM

From the lyrics of ABBA: "I'll cross the stream; I have a dream."

The life-challenging stories of great people like Abraham Lincoln and Nelson Mandela demonstrate that between you and your dream lies a stream to cross, and opposition to conquer. Between you and your destination lies a valley filled with disappointment, deception, derision, and denial. These great men gave their best and emerged the best, because they followed a course that was larger than the self and because they understood that, across the stream, people waited and yearned for their relevance.

Prepare yourself to cross the stream that separates you from your dream. You cannot realize a dream without opposition. Our faces, races, beliefs, norms, cultures, and desires may be different, yet we all have streams to cross. If your vision and your goals are strong enough, compelling enough, and worthy of your pursuit, you've got to cross that stream of opposition for your dream's actualization.

The reasons you must swim against the current of difficulty:

- Your celebration is across the stream, and people are waiting for you.
- You can help other people overcome their challenges, just as you did. Would you not like to be in a position of counselor to those in situations similar to what you went through? Experience counts.
- Swimming through the stream of difficulty brings out the best in you. As Johann Wolfgang von Goethe said, "Character develops itself in the stream of life."
- Your stream, in most cases, is the bridge between your ambition and its achievement.

It is time to prepare yourself emotionally and intellectually to deal with those factors that will compete against your dream. Learn from those who faced similar challenges. Learn how they swam their streams to get to their destinations. You are not your best until you swim your best.

PRINCIPLE #11: FALL BACK ON YOUR STRENGTH

Have you been out of work for so long that you don't know what to do next? Are you frustrated in your current career? Are you tired of working a job that isn't you? Are you tired of being disappointed by friends, family, colleagues, and employers? Do you feel like a disappointment to yourself? If you can answer any of these questions "yes," then it's time to look inward. It is time to fall back on your strength.

Fall back on your strength so you don't fall on the sword of frustration and fatigue. If your dreams remain unfulfilled indefinitely, there is no doubt the sword of disappointment will come—be it in the form of intolerable office politics, financial cutbacks, or even being laid off. In whatever shape or form the sword takes, don't let it divide you. Don't let it set you back. Don't sit back and succumb to fear or intimidation. Don't be trapped by worry and anxiety. Fall back on the talent that cannot be taken away from you.

Fall back on your strength. Your strength is a weapon against poverty, joblessness, and hardship—even in the midst of economic turmoil.

Fall back on your strength. Your strength is your security. Your skills, if properly developed, can secure your desired future. Your potential is the ultimate security against failure, frustration, and setbacks.

Fall back on your strength. Your strength is what you excel at. Don't let life bully you to a standstill. Fall back on your strength!

The P's and S's of strength:

- Your **progress** is in your strength; you gain **speed** in your place of strength.
- Your **provision** is in your strength; you gain the needed **supplies** in your place of strength.

- Your **promotion** is in your strength; you gain
  a **step** forward in your place of strength.
- Your **peace** is in your strength; you gain **serenity**
  resulting in confidence in your place of strength.
- Your **power** is in your strength; you gain
  superiority in your place of strength.
- Your **path** to ultimate fulfillment is in your strength;
  you gain **success** from a predefined destination that
  is in line with your goals in your place of strength.

Where does your strength lie? For many people, strength lies in the things they don't believe to be actual strengths; they see no real value in what they do well. They think inferior, and therefore feel inferior. Harboring an inferiority complex eats away at your confidence and hinders your ability to achieve. What a tragedy!

It's a tragedy because people who succeed are not better than you, only further down the road in understanding that you must search inward to discover your strength, and then develop and display it.

It is a tragedy because the road to self-recovery can be found in what you love to do. What you love to do is a clue to what you should be doing. Dr. Myles Munroe once explained:

> The wealthiest spot on this planet is not the oil fields of Kuwait, Iraq, or Saudi Arabia. Neither is it the gold and diamond mines of South Africa, the uranium mines of the former Soviet Union, or the silver mines of South Africa. Though it may surprise you, the richest deposits on our planet lie just a few miles from your house. They rest in your local cemetery or graveyard. Buried beneath the soil within the walls of those sacred grounds are dreams that never came to pass, songs that were never sung, books that were never written, paintings that never filled canvas, ideas that were never shared, visions that never became a reality, inventions that were never designed, plans that

never went beyond the drawing board of the mind,
and purposes that were never fulfilled. Our graveyards
are filled with potential that remained potential.

It is a tragedy to undervalue your own power to achieve greatness. It is a tragedy because undervalued strength lacks a competitive advantage. Don't undervalue your strength. Your strength may be small, but it can be developed to a higher level of fulfillment. Your strength may look crude, but it can be refined. Your strength may lack luster, but it can be polished and made to shine and be put to good use.

You are good at something that is of benefit to you and others. Find it. What can you fall back on when all else fails? Your sincere answer to this question may be the beginning of a purposeful life. Don't die faking it; live making it.

Advertise your strengths, not your weaknesses

People want to relate to your strength, not your weakness. Don't go about talking up your weaknesses; it doesn't do you any good. Tell the world what you are capable of doing, achieving, designing, and creating. This is what the world wants to hear. You are a burden to those to whom you play up your weaknesses. You shortchange your strength when you focus on how weak and incapable you are. You devalue your potential when you go about announcing what you can't do instead of what you can do. Why waste your precious time advertising your weaknesses when you can use that time to advertise your talent and skill?

If there are lessons to learn about strength, these include:

- Your respect is in your strength, not in your weakness.
- Your honor is in your strength, not in your weakness.
- It is your strength—not your weakness—that encourages you to endure the tunnel of despair and overcome your circumstances.

This is precisely why smart people don't advertise their weaknesses. It's time to starve your weakness and feed your strength—with the right stuff. Weakness doesn't sell; strength sells.

You are stronger than the challenges confronting you

Be the best you can be no matter the challenges that surround you. Challenges are frequent occurrences; we all face challenges at many points in our lives. Challenges come in various sizes and may be simple or complex. Some might be challenged by lack of access to adequate education, lack of business capital, or past failures resulting from bad decisions. Others might be challenged by physical problems, such as living with a disability or chronic illness. Challenges can make us feel inadequate, frustrated, and ashamed, and at worst, may prompt us to give up our dreams and desires.

Don't give up your dreams and desires no matter the challenges you face. Don't lose sight of a better tomorrow—the big picture. You are stronger than your challenges. You have what it takes to face challenges and turn them around. You have the power to take disadvantage and use it to your advantage, as well as the advantage of others.

Jean Sok, a dancer with only one leg, is a prime example of how our challenges can make us stronger if we do not give up trying. Watching Jean Sok dance on one leg with excitement, motivation, and energy reminds us that we can turn something seemingly impossible into an opportunity. It reminds us that "when the going gets tough, the tough get going."

It's time to change your perception about who you are, and the reasons why you avoid going after your dream.

Some facts about challenges:

- Your challenges are not designed to silence you; allow your voice to be heard.
- Your challenges are not designed to blind you; keep your eyes on the goal.
- Your challenges are not designed to repel you from the magnetic field of success; fight distractions.
- Your challenges are not designed to fence you off from achieving your goals and aspirations; step through the gate wearing your armor of courage.

Do not overvalue, or give too much power to, your challenges. Challenges are designed to be confronted and conquered. Your strength should consume your attention, not your weakness. The things you can do should consume your attention, not the things you can't do. You must not allow challenges to define you or dictate your worth. How you *respond* to challenge defines you and dictates your worth. Your dreams and desires are ahead of you, not behind.

PRINCIPLE #12: DEPART FROM THE WRONG ENVIRONMENT

In September 2011, a young Sei whale, which experts measured at thirty-three feet, died about 875 yards offshore near East Yorkshire Village, Skeffling, on the north bank of the Humber River in England. As physically powerful, huge, and energetic as this whale was, it could not survive in the wrong environment.

It is a tragedy to operate in the wrong environment. Are there not many today who aspire to be successful and yet operate in an environment which does not inspire them? How long will you stay in the place that stifles your inspiration and ability? How long will you remain devoted to the wrong course?

You are powerless in the wrong environment. No one maximizes the impact of their potential in an unfavorable environment. The wrong environment is toxic to your growth and hinders progress. The wrong environment is unfriendly terrain for anything of value you have to offer. Your struggles and frustrations are an indication that you are operating in the wrong environment; step beyond its oppressive boundaries.

Watch out for "VeViVu" Environments

VeViVu environments, or venom/vicious/vulture environments, squash dreams, place a barrier between you and your vision, and can stifle your desire to achieve your goals. The following is a breakdown of environments to avoid while working toward your dreams:

The venom environment: Depart from a low-level life. Harboring envy or jealousy for the things other people have that you don't creates an inhospitable and unproductive environment for working toward your goals. It is an environment that clouds your vision, belittles your capabilities, creates confusion, and generates unhealthy competition. The venom environment is cancerous to innovators.

The vicious environment: Do not create, embrace, or participate in violence.

Here are the reasons why:

- You can't operate in a violent environment and have *peace.*
- You can't operate in a violent environment and enjoy high-level *productivity.*
- You can't operate in a violent environment and make *progress.*
- You cannot be in a violent environment and foster *prosperity*.

Peace, productivity, progress, and prosperity require an environment devoid of violence in order to thrive. Resist and renounce violence and cruelty.

The vulture environment: Vultures prey on the weak; they feast on the rejected and the abandoned. Eagles and vultures do not flock together; they are opposites. To wait for or depend on others to do things for you, when you have the strength to influence your desires in a positive way, is to live in a vulture environment. Don't celebrate foolishness, folly, falsehood, or failure.

PRINCIPLE #13: FIGHT THE ENEMY WITHIN

The enemy within us is often the one we fail to see. The enemy of progress within you is much stronger than the one that exists outside of you. Many have been defeated, and many more will be defeated, by the enemy within. Internal enemies are like termites insidiously destroying the foundation of a beautiful and mighty structure. The problem with internal enemies is, like termites, they congregate and hide in your foundation, going unnoticed for too long. Before you know it, they've eaten away at your motivation to go after your dream.

Just as a foundation supports a building, your mind supports and determines the happenings around you. You are what you think. You are exactly how you see things. You cannot possess thoughts of failure, self-pity, inferiority, self-hatred, bitterness, envy, and jealousy and operate at your best. These are the internal termites I'm talking about. These enemies within must be defeated so you can think like a champion. They must be consciously chased out of your mind so that the best in you can grow and make a valuable impact on your generation. It's time to weed out the internal enemies and win the war within.

Here is why:

- Win the war within, and all other enemies will yield to you.
- Winning the war within creates relevance in your pursuit.
- Winning the war within creates happiness and self-confidence.
- Winning the war within brings out the best in you.
- Winning the war within qualifies you to
  mentor others in similar situations.

These are the wars you must first win before venturing out. Winning the wars on inferiority, self-pity, self-defeat, impatience, living an oversized life, procrastination, laziness, and discouragement are must-wins for your relevance, respect, recognition, and rewards.

Win the war on your inferiority complex

To feel and behave inferior is to not know who you really are and what you are capable of achieving—both for yourself and for humanity. The inferiority complex is one of the greatest enemies of achievement. It keeps you behind the success threshold of life. Feeling inferior prevents you from developing and demonstrating a high self- esteem.

Win the wars on self-defeat and self-pity

Self-defeat plus self-pity is a dangerous combination, culminating in anti-success and ineffective medication. Self-defeat and self-pity surging through your system creates toxicity. Neither will take you to the top.

Win the war on impatience

Impatience robs you of many valuable things. Imagine the things that could have been yours if you had simply waited and endured for just a little longer. Imagine goals you could have accomplished if you had just strived a little further.

Win the war on living larger than the self

Living an oversized life creates worry and anxiety. Anxiety leads to all kinds of pressure that often results in making irrational decisions. These termites create enormous holes in your foundation. Deal with them now, or they will gradually disintegrate what is left. Think larger than your pocket and spend less than is in your pocket.

Win the war on procrastination

How long will you permit the subtle enemy called "procrastination" to define you, dictate how far you'll go, deny your accomplishment of great things, and demote you to the camp of struggle? Fight this insidious little bug until it's completely demolished and can no longer identify you as its victim.

Win the war on laziness

You cannot sleep your way to success. Get up off the couch of unfulfilled dreams, which is full of broken springs and flat cushions. The further you sink into it, the more idleness and apathy define you. Roll out of the waterbed of unmet goals, which leaks. The longer you stay under the covers, the more chance you'll drown in anxiety and frustration.

Wake up and do something with your dreams. You cannot operate below your potential or your strength and be a happy person. Laziness is not a friend of success.

Win the war on discouragement

Surround yourself with an encouraging environment that speaks to your values. Surround yourself with people who inspire you. Visit the places where you consistently find encouragement. When places of encouragement are not to be found, encourage yourself.

Encourage yourself because:

- within you lies the ability to turn your current circumstances around;
- a step further can bring you to the level of life you have always desired;
- what is ahead of you is bigger, better, and more rewarding than the pain and failure of the past and present;
- others are waiting to hear you tell the story of how you overcame your challenges;
- when they count those who fought and won the battles over inferiority, self-pity, self-defeat, impatience, living an oversized life, procrastination, laziness, and discouragement, your name will be among those successful people.

PRINCIPLE #14: HAVE YOU TAKEN THE VOW OF EXCELLENCE?

A vow is an oath. In a court of law, an oath means that you've vowed to tell the truth. In the quest for excellence, taking an oath means remaining true to your vision, and to do and be your best at all times as you work to meet the goals that will accomplish your dreams. An outward manifestation of excellence is a reflection of the oath of excellence at work in those who possess it.

Your vow of excellence signifies:

- that you will strive to be the best you can be at all times;
- that you agree to gain mastery in your field of expertise;
- a conscious application to excellence in all of your undertakings;
- refusing to settle for average ratings in everything that you do; and
- refusing to give up your dreams, and agreeing to fight on in the face of intimidation, disappointment, fear, and despair.

When your vow of excellence is at work in all that you do:

- you cannot go unnoticed: you draw the attention of those who support and oppose you;
- you become uncommon: a symbol of respect;
- you become extraordinary: a step above the common position; and
- you become sought after: an instrument of relevance.

Several years ago during my undergraduate days, I tutored kids to support myself. One particular set of children I was privileged to teach were from a family where the father worked in design and printing—calendars, fliers, books, etc. He was a wealthy man who loved his job and was extremely talented at what he did.

I will never forget the day he sat me down in his office and taught me about the importance of total commitment to the cause one believes in. He said, "When people do not succeed, it is because they are not the best in what they do." He then said, "If I was a bus driver, I would strive to be the best and most popular bus driver on my route. If I was a cook, I'd strive to be the best, most sought after chef in the city."

This man had made the vow of excellence. I admired the attention to detail he applied to all facets of his job. It was no wonder big corporations and numerous institutions of learning awarded him generous contracts. Here was a man who told me that he'd never attended college because his family was too poor to pay for it. He taught himself computer applications such as AutoCAD, Corel Draw, Photoshop, and Excel. He strived for excellence and propelled himself to relevance by learning everything he could about what he wanted to do, and applied that knowledge daily to his work.

Excellence in what you do demands that you possess:

- a total and unwavering commitment in your assigned roles and responsibilities;
- a tireless learning habit; and
- effective time-management skills.

A full commitment to your roles and responsibilities requires a tireless learning habit—a hallmark of effective leaders. When you stop learning, you stop growing. When you stop growing, you may end up groaning. People of excellence keep their knowledge base up-to-date. I urge you to join the company of those who have sworn to soldier on in the pursuit of progress.

Effective time management skills translate to managing yourself well, managing the course to which you are committed, and managing your assigned roles and responsibilities.

I challenge you to take the vow of excellence in all that you do today!

PRINCIPLE #15: LEARN TO REFUEL

To refuel means to retreat, reassess your strategies, reprioritize, and renew your knowledge and information base. What is the beauty of an airplane if it can't fly you to your desired destination? The beauty of anything is in its ability to perform the function for which it was created. A person who refuses to regularly refuel is like a pilot failing to check the fuel gauge before takeoff and having to land the plane before it reaches its destination.

Regularly polish your communication skills by:

- consciously improving your interpersonal skills; and
- constantly updating your technical skills.

Time spent in refilling your gas tank is not time wasted. Things can go wrong when we do not regularly service our cars, and the same can be said of our knowledge and skills. To refuel is not to retire from pursuing your dreams. To refuel is to reflect, refresh, recuperate, and re-strategize. Reevaluate your goals and strategies to ascertain the potency of your dreams and aspirations.

Be vigilant in upholding the process of self-development. Self-development is an unending process from the cradle to the grave.

PRINCIPLE #16: EVERYTHING ABOUT YOU IS COMMUNICATING

That's right! Everything about you sends a signal. Whether you send a positive or a negative signal is up to you. In the moment you may not see the effect of negative communication, but it causes a ripple effect that accumulates over time. People begin to associate you with and define you by such traits.

To think you aren't communicating is naive. We all communicate on conscious and unconscious levels through our attire, hair, and attitude; verbally and non-verbally; formally and informally. Everything is communicating. The key to success is understanding that everything about you is communicating at all times.

You can't dress carelessly before an interview and not be noticed. You can't use a vulgar email address and not have it be noticed. As a professor, mentor, and life coach, I have, on numerous occasions, had one-on-one chats with my students about the negative signals that can be sent by way of an inappropriate email address. Why would an organization offer a job to someone whose email address sends a foul or disgusting signal?

PRINCIPLE #17: YOUR PICTURE IS YOUR FUTURE

The purpose of taking pictures is to keep your very best memories alive. The purpose of keeping your own picture in mind is to reenergize you and remind you that you are capable of achieving your dreams. The purpose of your total picture is to help you plan and plow, instead of plunge. The purpose of your total picture is to help you see what you can be so you can create a plan to become it.

Consider this:

- Your true picture becomes the ultimate source of your motivation. Motivation thrives on your ability to see what you are capable of becoming.
- Your true picture is your weapon against the average life. Not to recognize your potential is to settle for the average life.

- Your true picture is the surety against giving up too quickly. Most of us would have given up a long time ago if not for the total picture reminding us of what we can be.
- Your total picture shapes your behavior and defines your moral values.
- Your picture is your vision, and your vision dictates your values.

This is why:

- you cannot see your total picture and live in depression;
- you cannot see your total picture and not want to look like it;
- you cannot see your total picture and not want to live up to it; and
- you cannot see your total picture and not want to do everything in your power to become it.

People who have lost their wedding pictures, family albums, and the like understand how painful it is to lose precious memories of days gone by. They may cry or remain upset for long periods of time, wishing there was some way to get back what they've lost.

As painful as it is to lose photographs of precious memories, the most painful picture to lose is the picture of you. Here is where the problem lies. Many have lost the ultimate picture of themselves. They gave it up because of opposition they faced. They gave it up by choosing the path of least resistance. To lose the picture of who you can be and what you are capable of achieving is to lose a colorful future.

Watch out

Everything inside and outside of you will tempt you to give up the picture you have of yourself, therefore robbing you of your great future. Many more people would be doctors today had they not lost that picture of themselves and given up their dream for any number of reasons—lack of money, self-doubt, etc. Many more would be pilots today had they kept that picture of themselves in view and not merely settled for *wishing* to become a pilot. Think about what you could have been had you not given up. Think about what you would have achieved if you hadn't caved to distraction. The picture you have of yourself is to keep you from deviating from what matters most to you.

Many years back, during my undergraduate days as an engineering major, a classmate shared with me his compelling story about what it took for him to gain admission into the school of engineering. His ultimate dream was to become an engineer, specifically a top-level manager with a multinational corporation. It took this man five years to pass his entrance exam, an accomplishment that takes most people just a few months. But this man was so obsessed with his strong desire to be an engineer, he flat-out refused to be conquered by opposition.

I asked him why he never gave up and pursued something else. He said, "I've always had this image of myself as a successful engineer." His picture of himself as an engineer was his future, and he refused to settle for anything less. The picture of himself as an engineer became his driving force against opposition and compelled him to keep trying.

Friend, there is something about keeping a picture of what you can be. This picture may not be hung on a wall in your house or office, and friends and family may not even see it, but you know it's there because it reverberates in your head, unceasingly nagging at your thoughts to the point where it invades your mind. The total picture is what I term *the picture that won't give up on you.*

Holding onto the total picture of yourself in the face of challenges is your winning ticket against frustration and fatigue. Your picture is your future. Never exchange what you can be with less than who you should become. Relentlessly pursue the picture of greatness you have of yourself.

❝ Friend, there is something about keeping a picture of what you can be. This picture may not be hung on a wall in your house or office, and friends and family may not even see it, but you

know it's there because it reverberates in your head, unceasingly nagging at your thoughts to the point where it invades your mind. The total picture is what I term the picture that won't give up on you. **99**

The 5 P's of your picture

Your picture is more important than your **p**ast; it's your future. The power of your picture is to remind you that the best is still ahead of you. As bad and uninteresting as your past may have been, the future remains loaded with hope. Be optimistic about your future.

Your picture is more important than your **p**resent pain. No one enjoys the pain of the present. Your picture should remind you of what Robert Schuller said: "Tough times never last, but tough people do."

Your picture is more important than **p**eople's opinions. The voices of others can sometimes dissuade you from pursuing your dream. I have a friend in the IT industry whose parents wanted him to study medicine. From the beginning, his heart was in the world of technology. His parents knew where their son's passion lay, but, for whatever reason, they were adamant. Unfortunately, his parents' influence prevailed, and he eventually went on to medical school just to satisfy them. He excelled in medical school, but his heart wasn't in it—a waste of time and talent. During his second year in medical school, the picture of himself, which he'd buried securely inside of his heart when he'd agreed to become a doctor, drifted back into his mind. Against his parents' wishes, he dropped out of medical school to pursue his own picture of himself. His decision paid off: he is a happy, successful man. Somewhere in his heart, he understood that the picture he had of himself was bigger than the plan his parents had for him. Anything that can take your dreams, aspirations, and goals can deprive you of the future you've always dreamed about.

Your picture is worthy of your **p**ursuit. The story above shows that you cannot be happy looking away from your picture. Your picture is worth your attention. What is worth your attention is worth pursuing.

Your picture is your **p**assport to possibility, your roadmap to opportunity. People tend to become what they see. A law student sees herself as a lawyer before she becomes a lawyer. A medical student sees himself as a doctor before he becomes a doctor. Your picture is your inspiration to a world of possibility and opportunity. Your picture is your future. Whatever you see yourself as—an engineer, IT expert, mathematician, business tycoon, entertainer—you are capable of becoming it.

PRINCIPLE #18: REFUSED TO BE CLIPPED

Of what value is an eagle whose wings are clipped? As smart as eagles are, they are doomed without their wings. The glory of eagles rests in their wings. Simply put, to be clipped is to be caged. A clipped potential is a clipped future. What clips your potential?

Imagine an animal tethered to a pole. It can only move to the length provided by the rope to which it is tethered. You are limited by what you tolerate or permit to confine you. What tethers your ability to go after your dream?

While it's certain that the tides of discouragement and disappointment will roll in and out of your life, I challenge you to refuse to be pulled under. Rise above your circumstances. Ride above the waves that roar contrary to your moving forward.

Vow to remain unclipped by problems, pressure, pain, and poverty. Break the tether holding you back from your determination. Ride high on the wave of your dreams and aspirations.

PRINCIPLE #19: STRETCH YOUR HEART BEFORE YOU STRETCH OUT YOUR HAND

In the school of success, your heart is more important than your hand. The heart sustains the hand. Before your hand can reach for anything of value, that value must first live in your heart. The hand cannot receive what the heart has not conceived. Show me a heart that is void of conception, and I will show you an individual whose hand is void of reception.

The proof of payment in hand begins with a heart full of attainment. Don't underestimate the importance of the activities inside of you; they determine the happenings on the outside of you. Until you take care of what goes on inside, your outside expectations will remain elusive. It is disparaging for people to outstretch their hands to success without first having conceived that success in their hearts. This represents a misplaced priority. The hardcopy of success in your hand can only be accomplished through first conceiving a softcopy in your heart. The hand without the heart is a mockery of success, and the heart without the hand is simply daydreaming.

Your hand cannot get to where your heart has not reached.

Your ~~bea~~ work requires your heart.

> **66 The proof of payment in hand begins with a heart full of attainment. 99**

PRINCIPLE #20: YOUR PRESENT IS MORE IMPORTANT THAN YOUR PAST

To remain motionless in the fast lane is to be trampled. Not to stir up the potential inside of you is to resign yourself to defeat. Not to sharpen your skills through continuous improvement is to surrender to failure.

It's up to you to wake up or wail on. It's your responsibility to grow up or groan on. If you don't develop yourself now, you deny yourself the opportunity of tomorrow. You cannot live in your yesterday and remain relevant in your today. Today is more important than yesterday; your present is more important than your past.

CONCLUSION

A good intention requires great attention. I have written this book so you can:

- **R**ead and **R**espond
- **R**ead and **R**ecuperate
- **R**ead and **R**emember
- **R**ead and **R**evamp
- **R**ead and **R**ule
- **R**ead and **R**eign

Making decisions based on the information you have is more productive than gathering information without making decisions. It is not enough to be informed. ✓

Action cures.
Stop thinking. Act.

> **❝** *A good intention requires great attention.* **❞**

Information without transformation will keep you in the arena of frustration. Stacking up information without action will leave you stranded. By making sure your daily diary or to-do list is action packed, you'll be on your way to commanding results. Don't live an information-deprived life, and more importantly, don't live in a warehouse packed full of information without looking through the windows to see how to make that information work for you. Make up your mind to succeed. Leave behind whatever is holding you back, and focus on what will propel you forward.

You matter!

WHAT WILL YOU BE REMEMBERED FOR?

This is the soul-searching, soul-stirring question I want you to think deeply about. What you leave behind in this world is a question only you can answer.

How will you leave this world?
What will you leave behind?

Aspirations or Acrimony
Beauty or Blisters
Conqueror or Conquered
Dominion or Defeat
Energy or Exhaustion
Fruit or Fear
Gladness or Gloom
Heartiness or Heartaches
Inspiration or Insubordination
Joy or Junk
Keenness or Knocked aside
Laughter or Lukewarm
Merriment or Misery
Novelty or Nonsense
Optimism or Oddity
Peace or Problems
Quickened or Question mark
Revival or Regression
Success or Sorrow
Testimony or Trials
Uncluttered or Unruliness
Victorious or Victim
Wealthy or Wasted
Xenodochial or Xerothermic
Yeasty or Yoked
Zealous or Zapped

What will you leave as evidence worthy of emulation? What will you leave behind for the next generation? History will never forget people like Thomas Edison, who left us with the electric bulb; Alexander Graham Bell, the inventor of the first practical telephone; George Washington Carver, whose research provided alternative crops to cotton and three hundred uses for peanuts; Eli Whitney, inventor of the cotton gin; Mary Anderson, inventor of windshield wipers; Bette Nesmith Graham, inventor of liquid paper; Garrett Augustus Morgan, Sr., creator of a protective respiratory hood to save workers trapped in fume-filled tunnel systems; John F. O'Connor, inventor of **railway-draft gearing for connecting** locomotives to their framework; and Dr. Grace Murray Hopper, known for leading the team that invented the COBOL computer language.

All of these people passed the torch of possibility to the next generation. They each believed in their ability to create a better world, not only for themselves but for generations to come.

Neither can we easily forget modern-day inventors such as Dr. Philip Emeagwali, known for inventing the world's fastest computer; Sir Timothy "Tim" John Berners-Lee, a seasoned professor and the inventor of the World Wide Web; William Kamkwamba, the Malawian boy who harnessed the wind to generate electricity from scraps he handpicked from a junkyard; Jeff Greason of XCOR Aerospace, the frontier in commercial travel to space; Bill Gates, for his unprecedented technological breakthroughs in software and personal computers; Steve Jobs of Apple Computers, the pioneer of the personal computer revolution, commonly referred to as the Father of the Digital Revolution; Mark Zuckerberg of Facebook, a revolutionary in the world of internet social networking; Jeff Bezos, founder of Amazon.com, ardent entrepreneur, business revolutionary, and champion of the e-commerce industry; and Dr. David Oyedepo, Chancellor of Covenant University in Nigeria, who built the world's largest single auditorium, seating 54,200 under one roof, without foreign input on design or implementation.

The work of these successful people continues today in each of their names. They inspire hope.

We learn from these people because they weathered:

- **s**trife, to reach for higher heights of attainment;
- **t**horns and turbulence, to reach the zenith in their careers;
- **r**ejection, to emerge winners in pursuit of worthwhile dreams;

- **o**pposition, and still sailed through to the shore of possibility;
- **n**egativity and neglect, and still negotiated
  with their strength; and
- **g**roaning, yet cut through the barricade of limitations.

These great men and women became strong because they:

- **e**ndured by having dreams larger than the self;
- **n**ever gave up the picture of the future they so admired;
- **e**ncouraged themselves out of the depths of hopelessness;
- **r**efused to be clipped by challenges that confronted them;
- **g**rew and groomed themselves to greatness; and
- **y**earned for the best life offered in the face of
  seemingly insurmountable challenges.

These people proved that we are all capable of doing the impossible with the available. True visionaries want to give back to society. They want to solve problems. Think conceptually and proactively today. Don't sit back and criticize those doing their best. Hop on the train of innovation and problem-solving, and vow to leave the world a better place than when you arrived in it.

Dr. Derrick C. Samuels

Made in the USA
San Bernardino, CA
24 June 2019